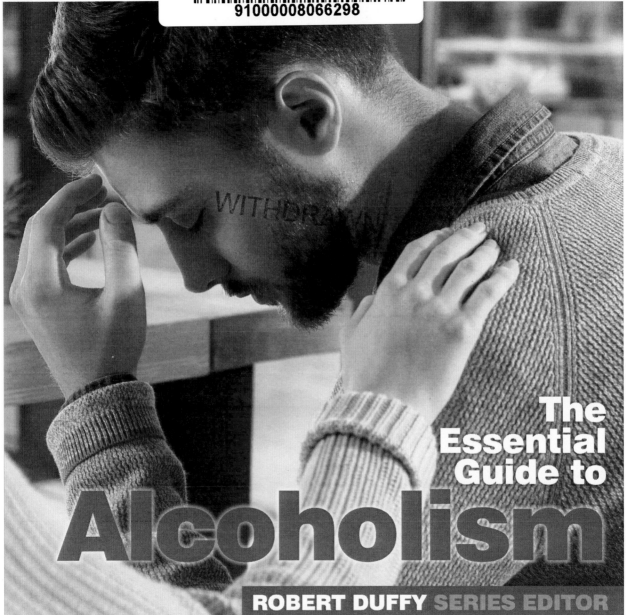

The Essential Guide to
Alcoholism

ROBERT DUFFY SERIES EDITOR

Published in Great Britain in 2019 by
need2know
Remus House
Coltsfoot Drive
Peterborough
PE2 9BF
Telephone 01733 898103
www.need2knowbooks.co.uk

SB ISBN 978-1-91084-392-5
Cover photograph: Adobe Stock

Contents

Introduction

Alcohol addiction (also known as *alcoholism* or *alcohol dependency*) is the world's number one drug problem, and has become dangerously common in the UK in recent years. Children and families suffer at the hands of the alcoholic and domestic violence is inextricably linked with its use. There are hundreds of thousands of people in the UK today who have a serious drink problem.

The chances are that you will definitely know at least one or two people who have a drink issue, maybe more. Why people become alcoholics is a hard issue to clarify. Its use ranges from the measured intake of the wine connoisseur to the desperate consumption by the street dweller of cheap cider or worse. You'll find alcohol in the majority of households across UK despite the fact that it's one of the most potentially damaging drugs available.

It's perfectly legal to purchase and consume (provided you're over 18), and is widely advertised across almost every form of media available. You'll likely think of "down-and-outs" huddled outside a drop-in centre or on the corner of the street when you try to picture an alcoholic. But the issue is far more widespread than you may think. Irresponsible drinking amongst young people is worryingly high, while the drink problems of adults and young people alike can take the form of anything from binge drinking on a Saturday night to acute stage alcoholism. While overall consumption has fallen by around 16% since 2004, the abuse of alcohol is the largest risk factor for death, disability and ill-health among 15-49 year olds in the UK, with drunk people continuing to fill A&E departments of hospitals 7 nights a week.

It's very possible that you could have a drink issue without even realising that the problem has reached that stage. In fact, the alcoholic is generally a highly skilled liar and it will often take some kind of crisis to really open their eyes. The biggest hurdle when tackling an alcohol issue is coming to terms with the fact that you have a problem. It really is a massive move forward.

But if it's you with the problem and you've picked up this book, you have made that frightening and so important first step by acknowledging there is an issue.

Growing up around people who drink heavily could contribute to someone's becoming an alcoholic, and so can simple bad luck. Research has also suggested that there could be a hereditary genetic weakness that can make some people more prone to alcohol dependency. Research proves that giving up is almost impossible without some kind of outside support, and I can't recommend enough that anyone dealing with this seeks counselling and medical advice as soon as possible.

It's an illness and needs to be understood as such.

Many people with alcohol dependencies will spend time pretending to both themselves and their loved ones that everything is fine. They may find themselves skirting around the issue, or making excuses for the various indicators they've found. Until someone is ready to admit that they have a problem, there's little that anyone can do to help them. You, yourself, can do nothing to change them; it has to come from them. Understanding this is very important if you're living with – or are closely acquainted with – an alcoholic.

Whether you have a problem or you suspect that someone close to you does, getting informed is a key part of the healing process and you're making a great start by picking up this book. It's time to take control and start living your life again, free of the suffocating and potentially fatal restrictions of alcohol dependence.

We hope that this book helps you to look at your options more clearly and reach a better understanding of the condition that you or your loved one may have.

This book is not designed to be your sole companion on your journey to a life free from alcoholism. It is not intended to replace professional medical advice. It's a very difficult process, and you'll need all the support you can get. What this book is designed to do is shine a light on to the path you are starting to tread by guiding you through the various support options and medical information that's available.

We aim to help those addicted and those who care about the sufferer to regain their freedom and stop suffering as a result of this illness. However this is affecting you, we hope that this book can help you along the way.

Disclaimer

This book has been written to give readers a basic understanding of alcohol dependency. Whilst every care has been taken to validate the contents of this guide up to the time of going to press, the author advises that he does not claim medical qualifications. Anyone with concerns is strongly advised to consult their GP. While this book can be used to support medical advice with a better understanding of the condition, it should not be used to diagnose or treat someone suffering from alcoholism.

Before undertaking any particular course of treatment, all readers are advised to speak to a qualified medical practitioner.

1

What is Alcohol Dependency?

The Facts

We need to pin down a clear definition of alcoholism before we can begin discussing any other aspect of the condition. First of all, true alcoholism is a form of disease. Also known as "Alcohol Dependence Syndrome", alcoholism is clearly defined in four ways: cravings, no control, physical reliance and capacity. It is not necessarily the person who had a heavy night on Saturday and overdid things.

It is a compulsive and progressive disease that can affect physical and mental health. For someone living with alcoholism, stopping is not simply a case of saying "No, thanks", and being reliant on alcohol is not something the sufferer has chosen. It can often interfere with things like work, family and relationships. There is a clearly defined difference between someone who enjoys a night out and sometimes has one too many, and an alcoholic.

The term "alcoholic" can be used a little too freely, and this can result in the difficult experiences of someone who suffers from alcoholism being erased and ignored.

Cravings

Thinking "Oh, I really fancy a cold beer" or "this food would really go with a glass of red wine" is fairly common – it's probably something that most of us will have thought at some point or other (and maybe even on a fairly regular basis). These thoughts are not the same thing as having a craving, though. It's a strong compulsion, a driving need to consume alcohol that overtakes everything else going on until the compulsion is satisfied. For an alcoholic, a craving is a completely overwhelming experience.

Lack of Control

The alcoholic will find it almost impossible to regulate moderate drinking, and almost certainly be incapable of switching to a soft drink, for example. Running out of booze is just not an option. For an alcoholic, losing control doesn't just mean drinking so much that you throw up or say something silly. It means that once you've started drinking, it's not possible to stop. They will continue to drink compulsively, with no control over their intake.

Physical Reliance

An alcoholic's body will become reliant on their alcohol intake – just as any other drug addict – and it will be necessary to drink continually in order to prevent them from feeling ill. Sweating, shakes, anxiety, paranoia and nausea are all common withdrawal symptoms in those giving up heavy and prolonged drinking. Often, the milder symptoms can be a regular daily occurrence upon waking, only relieved by drinking alcohol or by taking calming drugs such as beta blockers or diazepam. DTs, or delirium tremens, can occur in the most extreme cases, along with hallucinations and seizures.

> An alcoholic's body will become reliant on their alcohol intake – just as any other drug addict – and it will be necessary to drink continually in order to prevent them from feeling ill.

Alcohol Tolerance

Aside from the physical dependence of drinking just to stop feeling dreadful, the alcoholic is also seeking that elusive 'high' – and as time goes by, the quantity of alcohol needed to achieve that increases. Someone who is accustomed to drinking large amounts will need a larger amount of alcohol than someone who does not often drink if they wish to feel the effects of inebriation.

It's not about having a discerning palate - it's about the end result. It's more important to them than eating and will take first place over children and family, work, friends or even the alcoholic's own well-being. Many people with an alcohol dependency are not fussy about what they drink. Alcohol is expensive, so in order to afford the large quantities they require, many will stick with cheap lagers and may even resort to drinking alcohol that wasn't intended to be drunk (like wine that was bought for cooking and has been open for some time).

All of this means that someone who is dependent on alcohol will find it very difficult to kick their addiction. It's far more complex than simply drinking less or taking up a new hobby. This is a disease that can consume a person.

Other Drink-Related Conditions

Alcohol dependency is a debilitating disease in its most classic form. However, drink problems can come in a number of other forms.

Binge-Drinking

The binge drinker is usually a habitually moderate drinker during the week, but goes on wild benders at the weekend. It also leaves the drinker open to spiking, as they lose control of what's going on around them. This type of drinking is often used by shy or anxious people to boost their confidence in social situations, and is very common in teenagers and young people (especially women).

It can result in huge financial outlay, memory blackouts, unprotected casual sex and fighting, as well as place huge strain on the liver and the body as a whole. For more information about binge drinking, read the case study later in the book.

Underage Consumption

While the number of young people drinking in the UK appears to be slowly declining, it is still at an alarmingly high rate with 15% of 11 year olds and 73% of 15 year olds admitting to taking part in underage drinking. The rise of the 'alcopop' has made the products more palatable to younger taste buds and children as young as nine or 10 have been reported turning up for school drunk.

With higher numbers of teenagers having access to make-up and clothing that makes them appear older than they are, it's becoming ever-easier for them to purchase alcohol in pubs and shops without an adult's assistance.

Foetal Alcohol Syndrome

Foetal Alcohol Syndrome can occur if a pregnant person drinks often and continuously throughout their pregnancy, something which people do all too often. Heavy continuous drinking or binge drinking throughout pregnancy can have a profound effect on unborn children, leading to premature and underweight babies, with skeletal and neurological weaknesses. A very occasional glass of wine isn't going to be the end of the world, but any more than that can lead to very serious issues. We'll discuss this issue in greater detail in Chapter 6.

Alcohol Poisoning

Fast drinking slows down reactions and as the body becomes incapable of processing the intake, the brain stops being able to govern the body properly. Alcohol poisoning is a serious issue most commonly seen in people who tend to engage in binge drinking. If you encounter someone who you believe has alcohol poisoning, you should put them in the recovery position and call 999. Signs to watch out for include clammy skin, loss of bladder control, slow and laboured breathing, unconsciousness and vomiting.

Dual Addiction

In many cases, people with an alcohol addiction will also be addicted to other things. In some cases this will be an addiction to heavy drugs like amphetamines and cocaine, while in others it could be a simple smoking addiction. If drugs are involved, it's a good idea for the individual to try and treat their drug and alcohol addictions at the same time, as the effects of alcohol can make the high produced by drugs like cocaine much more intense. Trying to just give up one will never really work.

Know the Difference

These conditions – whilst being a definite cause for concern – are largely self-inflicted, and if daily, compulsive drinking is absent where some of these other behavioural patterns are seen, then you are probably looking at an alcoholic. However, many of the behavioural patterns listed above are likely to be present in someone with an alcohol dependency, and this can be a little confusing. The majority of alcoholic individuals will need help, support and treatment to recover from their disease.

It may seem like self-indulgence to the observer, but the alcoholic needs treatment in the same way as any other sufferer from disease. A true alcoholic – someone who relies on compulsive daily drinking – is at far greater risk of destruction than someone who is, for example, prone to occasional binge-drinking.

Some people with alcohol dependency will be able to recover without help, but they are in the minority. It's not simply a case of will-power, so cases where someone has fully recovered all on their own are very uncommon.

Is it Inherited?

There is a propensity for the children of alcoholics to become vulnerable to the same condition as their parent. If you had alcoholic parents, it's a wise precaution to be aware of the higher chances of your own susceptibility, but be careful to draw the line between being aware and living in fear. There is more about this issue in Chapter 3.

Alcohol addiction is believed to be hereditary, so the short answer to this question is "yes". That said, a person's likelihood of following in the footsteps of a parent with alcohol dependency is also impacted by a range of risk factors, so it's not set in stone. Environmental issues will affect the outcome too, as will peer group behaviour and the availability of alcohol – in fact all these things can contribute.

It's not a simple case of whether or not a certain code is "in your blood" when it comes to alcohol addiction. It's perfectly possible for someone to have a completely healthy relationship with drink, even if their parent was addicted. Just be careful and try not to become negatively obsessed with alcohol, as this may cause you to create a self-fulfilling prophecy.

Some people with alcohol dependency will be able to recover without help, but they are in the minority.

What Happens Without Recovery?

Alcohol addiction is a gradual degenerative disease which can eventually become fatal if left untreated. The good news is that it's treatable, providing the alcoholic is prepared to face up to the problem. A death from alcohol abuse is not a pleasant one. There is no such thing as the "odd drink" for an alcoholic. The only way to move forward is total abstinence, and this makes recovery a very difficult, rocky journey.

The following table shows the number of alcohol-specific deaths in the UK from 2002-2017.

Year	Males rate per 100,000 population	Females rate per 100,000 population
2002	16.8	7.9
2003	17.8	8.1
2004	17.6	8.3
2005	17.9	8.3
2006	18.3	8.8
2007	17.0	7.7
2008	17.8	7.9
2009	16.3	7.6
2010	16.8	7.4
2011	16.7	7.7
2012	15.2	7.2
2013	15.5	7.1
2014	15.7	7.4
2015	15.4	7.5
2016	16.2	7.5
2017	16.8	8.0

Data taken from the Office for National Statistics, www.ons.gov.uk.

Summing Up

- The alcoholic feels like they cannot live without the drink.

- Liver damage, heart disease, coronary attack, confused or anxious mental state and risk of cancer are all dangers for the chronic alcoholic.

- There is no "odd glass of wine" for the alcoholic.

- People who have an alcohol dependency or addiction are very different from those who are only social and occasional drinkers, or even binge drinkers.

- If there's no alcohol available, a person with an alcohol addiction will do whatever it takes to get some, as it will consume all of their attention until they do.

- Until they are able to have a drink, the individual is likely to display physical symptoms like uncontrollable shaking or an inability to eat.

- Giving up drinking will reverse a lot of the damage done by years of alcohol abuse.

- Someone who was previously addicted to alcohol will not be able to simply "have a drink", even after they've kicked the habit.

2

Spotting the Problem

What Does Alcoholism Look Like?

I f you think you are an alcoholic or alcohol abuser, or you suspect someone else might be, there are some fairly standard signs to look out for. Nothing in your life will be as important as your desire for alcohol if you have an alcohol addiction. If you have an alcohol *dependency*, the need will be slightly less severe, though you may feel as though you won't be able to deal with situations like shyness or stress without a drink.

Binge drinking, underage drinking and similar issues will then fit into the category of alcohol *abuse*.

Are You an Alcoholic?

Some people reading this book may be worried about themselves. If that's you, try taking this quiz, remembering to think about your answers carefully. Just tick all the statements you feel apply to you, and count up your total.

If it's not yourself you're concerned about, you can easily apply the questions to someone else.

Are You an Alcoholic?

- Do you use alcohol to distract you from other issues?
- Have you ever gotten drunk on your own?
- Does drinking ever make you feel embarrassed or guilty?
- Has drinking ever caused you to miss work?
- Do you have a reputation for drinking a lot?
- Do you feel the need to understate the amount you drink when talking to other people?
- Do certain times of day make you crave a drink?
- Has a doctor or clinician ever treated you for drinking?
- In the last year has a relative or friend, or a doctor or other health worker been concerned about your drinking or suggested you cut down?
- Has drinking ever resulted in you being admitted to an institution or hospital, including A&E?
- Do you want a drink when you wake up?
- Has drinking made you lose interest in your career?
- Does drinking make you thoughtless about your family?
- Is drinking affecting your home life?
- Have you ever had a loss of memory as a result of drinking?
- Do you often have six or more units at one time?
- Do you drink because you are shy?

It's easy to drift along, thinking that everything is okay, and hiding from the issue. The more yeses, the bigger the issue. An alcohol problem of some form is definitely indicated if you're able to answer yes to four or more of these questions. These questions have been carefully constructed to highlight problem areas, however much control you feel you have over your drinking. You should definitely take a closer look at your relationship with alcohol if you've answered "yes" to a few of the questions.

Does Someone You Care about Have a Drinking Problem?

The quiz below is based on one devised by Al Anon, a family support body set up to help those who are affected by someone else's drinking. Whether it's alcohol abuse, alcohol dependence or alcoholism, the chances are you know at least one person either at home, at work or in your social circle who has a drink problem. It's more common to have a drinking problem than many people would believe.

Your parents, for example, could have one without you ever having realised it. This quiz can give you a good indication of whether the person you're thinking about has a drinking problem or not.

Does Someone You Care about Have a Drinking Problem?

- Have you been upset about your parent, close friend or relative's drinking?
- Are family holidays and special occasions frequently ruined by alcohol?
- Do you hate spending time in your house and stay away when possible?
- Does it feel like alcohol is more important than your feelings and wellbeing?
- Does the drinker's behaviour seem to be triggered by you, your family or friends, or just life as a whole?
- Is someone else's drinking causing financial issues in your life?
- Has drunken behaviour ever made you consider contacting the police?
- Are there other problems in your life that you feel would be solved if the drinker didn't drink anymore?
- Have you refused dates out of fear or anxiety?

Whether it's alcohol abuse, alcohol dependence or alcoholism, the chances are you know at least one person either at home, at work or in your social circle who has a drink problem.

- Are meal times frequently delayed because of the drinker?
- Do you believe no one could possibly understand how you feel?
- Are you afraid or embarrassed to bring your friends home?
- Are you afraid to upset someone for fear it will set off a drinking bout?
- Do you tell lies to cover up for someone else's drinking or what's happening in your home?
- Do you cover up your real feelings by pretending you don't care?

For further information, contact Al-Anon Family Groups Headquarters, 1600 Corporate Landing Parkway, Virginia Beach, VA 23454-5617, USA. Tel: (757) 563-1600, **www.al-anon.org**. The help list at the back of the book looks in greater detail at the support groups and help options available, both online and in person.

There is a definite cause for concern if you have answered "yes" to three or more of the questions above.

It's up to the drinker to face his or her problem and deal with it. It is never going to be easy to deal with a drinking problem, whether it's your own or someone else's. It's especially common to feel helpless if it's someone else who has the drinking problem.

It's not all bad news, though! You're not alone in living with someone who abuses alcohol. There are loads of great support groups out there, full of people who will understand the situation you're in.

The most important thing you can do right now is to find somewhere you can talk to other people about what you're going through. It will make a huge difference in the way you cope. According to research, the issue will become much easier to deal with if you're getting help and advice from other people.

Affecting Your Life?

It's very hard to watch a dearly loved friend or family member destroying himself or herself in this way. What is harder to understand is the behaviour that goes with it: lying to cover the habit, putting everything else further down on the list of priorities and, of course, the drunken behaviour itself. Drinking problems affect everyone who cares about the drinker, not just the person with the addiction.

In fact, an alcohol addiction is often more distressing for the drinker's loved ones. Even if the person with the addiction is just a colleague of yours, it can still have a big impact on your life if you always find yourself covering for sloppy work, poor time management or long lunches.

If you go out with someone who has an alcohol problem you'll likely notice that they can become tearful and quiet or aggressive and disagreeable. You will also notice their capacity for drink is way beyond anyone else's – they can drink an awful lot and still stand up. They may drink much more quickly than your other peers, and their behaviour may become inappropriate.

Drinking problems may be quieter in the home. Even without a pub atmosphere, though, drinking can lead to irrational behaviour, disputes and violence. It's not much fun, especially if it's your mum or dad. It can be very difficult to live with someone with an alcohol addiction.

If it's you who has the drinking problem, you may be aware of all this deep down. And knowing all of this hurtful stuff can make giving up even harder, because it can make you feel really worthless. It's hard not to take it all personally, but alcoholism is an illness and needs to be treated as such. Whether you're the person drinking or the person who's affected by the drinker, it's important to keep in mind that it is not on purpose, and it is nobody's fault.

Summing Up

- You could easily have a drinking problem without even realising it – these issues are far more common than a lot of people may think.

- Taking the quizzes will certainly help to highlight any issues, and may prove to be a wakeup call, whatever your situation.

- Denial and avoidance are key in this insidious illness, and facing it will definitely be a positive move.

- Often, the biggest step is realising that there is a drink problem to address in the first place.

3

Families and Alcohol

Is It Hereditary?

I f you're a person with an alcoholic parent then you already run a high risk of developing the condition yourself. Alcoholism can be hereditary – this much we know for sure. That said, this isn't an excuse to ignore the issue and "accept the inevitable" as it takes more than just genetics for you to develop the condition. It does mean, however, that you will need to be more self aware than other people.

You won't necessarily become an alcoholic just because you have a slightly elevated likelihood of becoming one. Keep in mind that there are three main factors that can come into play here.

Genetics

Genetics are partly responsible for the fact that alcohol addictions tend to run in families. The current popular opinion is that it's the genetic anomaly, coupled with the environment and learnt behaviour that creates an alcoholic. Research sourced from NIAAA Alcohol Alert also shows that identical twins who are the offspring of an alcoholic parent and who live separately without knowledge of each other have both developed alcoholism independently.

What we know for sure though is that it's more than just something "in your blood". Since 1989, the NIAAA (National Institute on Alcohol Abuse and Alcoholism) have funded the Collaborative Studies on Genetics of Alcoholism (COGA) to try and find out which specific genes are connected with alcoholism. In addition, NIAAA funds investigators' research in this important field, and also has an in-house research emphasis on the interaction of genes and the environment.

Unfortunately, we can safely say that the children of alcoholics will have a harder time avoiding alcoholism than those who grew up in homes without alcohol addiction.

Unfortunately, we can safely say that the children of alcoholics will have a harder time avoiding alcoholism than those who grew up in homes without alcohol addiction.

Environment

Environmental issues can play a huge part in developing a drink problem. As we've already discussed, alcohol addiction is about more than just genetics. An unhappy childhood can have a great influence over future behaviour. The children of people with drinking problems tend to achieve less well at school than they should, suffer from anxiety and live with pervasive tension and disorder at home.

Learnt Behaviours

If all a child has ever known is habitual heavy drinking and unreasonable behaviour, it's going to be hard for them to realise that's not the normal way to live. Bad habits and learnt behaviour are the final contributing factor to the development of a drink problem. It may be difficult to avoid falling into habits seen at home while growing up, and adjusting to life outside of this family and away from the behaviours associated with alcohol abuse will be a real challenge.

At the end of the day, all three of these factors play a major role in deciding whether you will or will not develop an alcohol addiction or dependency. If you happen to be the child of an alcoholic, avoiding this path will require that you be extra careful about your environment and behaviours.

need2know

Case Study: Alan

Alan is an alcoholic now in his early forties. He says that the environment he grew up definitely contributed to his addiction: his mother was an alcoholic, too. But rather than admit to there being a problem with her drinking, she used to look for different excuses.

Alan explains: "I could never bring home friends, it was too embarrassing. Every day I could come home from school and it wasn't like, would she be drunk, it was like, how drunk will she be? She used to drink a lot when I was younger, that's all I really remember. My dad didn't know what to do, he couldn't stand it. So he'd either be furious, trying to stop her, or he'd just be there.

"There was less awareness about alcohol abuse in the seventies than there is now, and looking back I'd definitely say that he felt completely helpless. I remember hearing their arguments from upstairs, and it really made me feel sick. To be honest, I preferred it when he wasn't around."

Alan and his younger sister were always blamed for their family's problems.

"It was a real case of her feeling like 'I could have been someone', except that all the reasons for her not being whatever she wanted to be were in her head. Sometimes it was even impossible to do homework – she'd appear in your bedroom, shouting and crying. I used to avoid going home for as long as possible every day, and I couldn't stand the mess everywhere. I wanted so much to get away.

"She often pointed the blame at us when she was crying. She'd tell us all about how unhappy she was, and how it was because of my father and us. She hated everything but the alcohol. Of course, she'd be completely drunk. She was hammered every day of the week. If it wasn't for that, she really could have achieved whatever she wanted. I didn't mind so much when I was very young, but by the time I was a teenager I just felt really ashamed.

"I was terrified my school friends would find out what my family was like. I avoided ever discussing it with anyone, because I was sure everyone would gossip about me at school.

"My younger sister and I would have to sort out things like food – by the time I was around 11 my mother had stopped bothering with cooking and stuff. It was a real mess."

Alan says that his mother encouraged him to try alcohol from an early age, and sometimes even bought drinks because she thought he and his sister would like them. His own addiction, he feels, probably stemmed from this. He has admitted that he has no children because he didn't want to put them through what he and his sister went through, which is terribly sad.

"Fancy giving kids alcohol just to make yourself feel better about your own drinking. I can see now that she was looking for someone to share her complicity so she wouldn't feel so guilty, but looking back, it makes me so very, very angry. Things like alcopops weren't around in those days, so she'd buy sweeter drinks like Dubonnet and mix them with lemonade so we could drink them. If I'm honest, I don't think I ever stood a chance. An addiction makes you selfish and unreasonable, it's a very powerful thing."

Alan was just 17 when his mother died, and he says it was a bit of a relief even if it was very sad. She'd been sober a few times for very brief periods, mostly just when she'd been hospitalised because her body couldn't take any more. But she'd always be drinking again before too long. Her heart was never in it.

Alan understands that he has a problem and is trying his best to face it. That's the biggest difference between him and his mother. He is trying to be practical about the issue.

"I didn't really notice my drinking, until suddenly I realised my life was falling apart. I was finding that I was getting to around lunchtime and starting on the booze. I have a better understanding of how she felt now, so in a weird way I have more sympathy for her. You have no idea what it's like unless you can stand in my shoes. I manage a bar and a B&B where I make the breakfasts each morning. I'm not at a desk with people looking over me all day – I'm working for myself.

"Then I realised that actually, if I didn't have a drink first thing in the morning, I wouldn't be able to get through the day without being really shaky. I can't sleep properly, I can't eat first thing until I've had a few beers or I throw up, and my bowel movements are best not talked about, frankly. I realised that I'd started drinking earlier and earlier each day. I have issues with anxiety, and was using the alcohol to take the edge off.

"Last year I worked up enough courage to have my first holiday away from the B&B for a few years and had to pretty much get blotto to event tackle it. When we got there, I discovered that the place we were staying was miles away from the nearest shop that sold alcohol. I had to get my wife to get up at 5AM to drive me to that shop so we could wait for it to open.

"In the car, I was terrified. I sat there shaking until the shop opened and I could get a drink. When I got my hands on it, I didn't even drink that much. I just needed to know I had it if I needed it, and being without it was the most terrifying thing I've ever experienced. I was petrified – sobbing uncontrollably in the car, and I couldn't stop shaking.

"I never saw it coming, and before I knew it I had the same stupid problem my mother had."

Right now, Alan is working towards giving up alcohol. He's finding it really hard, and openly admits that the idea terrifies him.

"I'm not sure if my agoraphobia has been caused by my drinking or just made worse by it, but either way it's a massive problem. Since that awful holiday away from the B&B, I've been working hard to sort out this addiction. But I'll be first to tell you, I'm scared to death. I know I hit rock bottom that day."

Alan believes that the best way for him to quit is to gradually reduce the amount he drinks before stopping completely. He hopes that will soften the blow a little. He often backslides and needs to start again, cutting back gradually. It's a real struggle, and his current goal is to make it to the afternoon before having his first drink.

"I guess I'm putting it off but I really am trying, and at least I'm making a difference, however small. This process is dragging on a bit," Alan confesses. "I think I'll need to put some sort of time limit on it. But I can't go to AA until I quit and I am just too scared to give up totally just yet. The doctor has given me some beta-blockers to help with my anxiety, and I have a friend I can talk to when it gets too much.

"I'm making a promise to myself never to end up the same as my mother did. I'm going to get there, eventually."

All names in case studies are changed to protect the speaker's identity.

Living with an Alcoholic

Alcoholics will often blame everyone but themselves for the problems they create, and until there is some kind of crisis – usually a sort of breakdown on the part of the alcoholic – the greatest issue will be denial. As Alan's experience demonstrates, drinking alcohol alters behaviour and this can be happening on a daily basis, changing the personality of the drinker.

It's also a sad fact that abuse, both sexual and physical, is a high risk factor in alcoholic homes – this can be aimed at children or partners. Work is normally affected, with the drinker even losing jobs and there is generally a financial burden. Bodily functions are affected, as are sleep patterns, and it's not unusual for sleepwalking, coupled with urinating in the wrong places, to be common.

Social embarrassment is high on the list of worries – drinkers will often let themselves down by behaving badly and the social invites will dry up. It'll be hard for anyone who has not lived with someone who abuses alcohol to understand what it's like to endure this family disease. It's difficult to understand how something as simple as a drink can cause someone you love to transform into a different person entirely.

As Alan's experience showed, those living with such a person will feel completely helpless. Home life can slowly become unhappy and uncomfortable as holiday after holiday is ruined by rows and inappropriate behaviour. A person who is addicted to alcohol can quickly lose track of things like homemaking and cleaning. Above all else, an alcohol addiction can place a massive emotional drain on the drinker and those who care about them.

A vast percentage of domestic violence cases are linked to alcohol abuse, with violence and disputes becoming frequent occurrences. Many people with alcohol dependency will feel the need to lie about their control over their drinking habit, and can become upset if pressed on the matter. Many will try to hide evidence of their intake.

In Hot Water

The experience of living with an alcoholic can be simplified into an analogy for those who don't understand where you're coming from. Think about what would happen if you climbed into a bath filled with water that was way too hot. It'd hurt, and you'd jump right back out because it was unpleasant. However, if you got into a bath that was a comfortable temperature and slowly added hot water until it was the same high temperature, you'd probably stay put because it wouldn't be so noticeable. Living with alcoholism is a bit like that. The trouble with living with alcoholism is that you don't detect the creeping heat until suddenly, without noticing, you're sitting in a bath of water that's far too hot.

A person who abuses alcohol can behave in ways you'd never put up with at the start of the relationship. But alcoholism is a very gradual disease, and it's easy for these negative behaviours to sneak up on you without you even noticing how bad they are.

The best place to find understanding is amongst others who live or have lived with similar situations. This is why support groups are so important to those living in this damaging and upsetting situation.

Why Me?

More often than not, a person with an alcohol addiction will be very unhappy because of their condition. The people living and working with them suffer too, and especially if you're a child living in this situation it's really hard not to wonder if it's your fault. Blaming either yourself or them will not help. It's a complex condition affected by genetics, environment and heredity.

The drinker is the only person that can make a difference to their drinking patterns. It's vital that we keep in mind that nobody develops an addiction for the fun of it. They drink because they can't help it, not because they particularly enjoy it.

It's easy to slip into the belief that things would change if you'd done something differently.

These beliefs aren't useful or healthy.

You'll need to try your hardest not to feel like changing things is your job, and not to take their behaviour personally. This is absolutely not your fault, and there's nothing you could have done that would have stopped this. And although it may feel very much like it is, this isn't the fault of the person with the addiction either. For now, all you can do is be there for them when they are ready to change their life, and care for yourself by seeking support from others who have experienced something similar.

Blaming either yourself or them will not help. It's a complex condition affected by genetics, environment and heredity.

The Role of the Enabler

It is possible to be living with someone with an addiction and to accidentally help them to continue their self abuse. Perhaps you've lent them money or paid their bills for them. Your actions are well intentioned, usually meant to help or support, but you could be enabling the continuation of the problem. While you need to understand that someone's alcohol addiction cannot be your fault, it's also important to make sure that you aren't enabling their destructive behaviours.

When your partner was too hung over to go to work, have you ever helped them out by calling in "sick" on their behalf? Or have you threatened to leave, more than once, but stayed put? Have you invented ways to excuse their behaviour? Have you ever tried to make their drinking seem okay by drinking yourself to create the illusion of social drinking?

Enabling patterns tend to fall into three main categories. Actions like this need to be looked at carefully – while they're meant well, all they do is enable the person's addiction.

The Saviour

If you're working hard to maintain some semblance of normality, or find yourself rushing to help out the person with the addiction, you may fall into the "Saviour" category. These heroic efforts mean that the drinker can go about feeling that it's all okay. This type will cheerfully make breakfast in the morning without a word about what went on the night before. They will lie to cover the alcoholic's actions. They'll be there to catch their drunk friend when they fall, give them a pillow and a blanket when they pass out on the couch, and clean up whatever mess they've made. They protect the person from the consequences of their actions by working to make everything appear okay. Getting help isn't going to happen, because the person with the addiction won't see that something's gone wrong.

The Sufferer

The Sufferer will feel the burden of the situation very heavily and will often be in tears, making heartfelt whispered telephone calls to friends for support, but saying little to the alcoholic. It's a destructive downward spiral that does nothing except distract everyone from the real problem.

The Sufferer's plan is to try and guilt the person with the addiction into changing through the magic of guilt tripping. In reality, this pattern of behaviour will do nothing but give the person with the addiction something to think about other than themselves, as the sufferer becomes increasingly depressed and distant. The behaviours of both parties will gradually become even worse as the drinker becomes frustrated by the Sufferer's imaginary superiority, and arguments and punishments may result.

The Aggravator

The Aggravator tries to change behaviour by threatening to leave or by using a constant stream of anger and resentment, hoping in the end it will get through. This course of action usually only serves to drive the drinking further underground. Of the three types, the Aggravator is the angriest. They will berate and mock the person with the addiction as they are angry about their behaviour, and will often get worked up and shout about it.

To gain extra support, the Aggravator will often get other people involved in the arguments and the house will become increasingly unpleasant to be in. This fighting is just another distraction from the real issues, and it will be very difficult for anyone with an alcohol addiction to find the headspace or motivation to stop with all this rage in the air.

Children's reactions tend to be more instinctive, of course, so their behaviour rarely matches any of these patterns. As the alcoholic looks for yet another excuse, the child will find themselves blamed for the situation.

How Do I Stop the Patterns?

Any kind of collusion, whether it's mopping up after them or giving them something else to think about, such as an argument, will only detract from their self analysis. Although, as I've said, you cannot realistically change the alcoholic, you can do something to help. We promise that, however difficult things may seem, there is still hope. Of all the things you could do now, doing nothing is probably your best option.

If they're looking for an argument, don't rise to it; if they can't get out of bed in the morning, don't let it affect your own routine. Of all your limited options, refusing to react to what's happening around you is probably the most positive thing you can do. Eventually, having to face their issues alone will create motivation for them to accept reality.

When you stop making it your problem, it'll become clearer that the person does have a problem and that they have to deal with it. Give them the space to go about asking for help.

Summing Up

- Alcoholism is a family disease. This phrase is used all the time – because it is so accurate.

- As we saw in Alan's story, one person's addiction can become everyone's problem.

- While it's not an unavoidable problem, it's important to keep in mind that there is a genetic factor that can affect someone's predisposition towards inheriting alcoholism.

- Growing up with that can have a profound effect on a person, so it's no wonder the children of alcoholics are changed by this.

- If you think you might have a drinking problem, try to pay attention to what's going on around you and what issues you are creating.

- It is responsibility of the person with the addiction to break the habit and take back control of the situation.

- Anyone who's reading this book and has got this far is highly likely to be in a receptive state – you wouldn't be reading it otherwise!

- And, therefore, you stand a good chance of finding an alternative to the destructive path of alcoholism.

- If you're living with the alcoholic, try not to assume those roles that make it hard for them to face their problems.

- Whoever is suffering from the condition will affect all those around them, causing turmoil and friction.

4

Teenage and Underage Drinking

Young People and Drinking

Alcohol addiction is rarely seen in anyone younger than 30, so it tends to be viewed as a problem for older people. Teenage drinking is well-documented in the press these days; the rise of binge drinking amongst young people and the proliferation of underage drinking make for shocking headlines. Alcohol problems are not confined to the older generation, though it does take a few years for true alcoholism to become a full-blown condition.

The headlines published by newspapers only highlight a small part of a very real problem.

In 2003, a survey carried out by the BBC and the British Association of Accident and Emergency Medicine found that binge drinking on alcopops had resulted in the hospitalisation of children as young as six. The Corporation's study of 50 A&E departments found that in one unit alone, as many as 100 drunken children one week were seen, and 70% of staff believe that child admissions are consistently getting younger.

More recently, a report from the Health and Social Care Information Centre found that 13,725 young people aged under 18 were admitted to hospital with alcohol related problems between 2011/12 and 2013/14.

Having a Good Time?

Getting completely wasted, for many young people, is the definition of having a good night out. Although things are very slowly improving, it's not happening quickly enough and the number of teenage and even younger drinkers who engage in binge drinking is deeply alarming. For statistics, see the table below.

How Much Do Young People Drink?

Average alcohol consumption in units, according to pupils in England who had drunk in the last week (by gender and age) – 2000 to 2016.

	2000	2002	2004	2006	2008	2009	2010	2011	2012	2013	2014	2016
All Pupils All ages	10.4	10.6	10.7	11.4	16.0	11.6	12.6	11.3	13.3	8.4	10.6	10.3
Aged 11-13	6.4	6.8	7.8	10.1	12.0	8.7	12.1	6.8	7.7	(4.3)	(5.5)	6.9
Aged 14	9.8	10.3	9.9	10.9	15.1	10.4	11.0	9.4	16.5	8.8	11.3	11.1
Aged 15	12.9	13.0	12.9	12.3	15.5	13.2	13.9	11.7	12.3	8.7	10.0	9.8
Boys All ages	11.7	11.5	11.3	12.3	16.0	11.6	12.6	11.3	13.3	8.4	10.6	10.3
Aged 11-13	8.3	7.3	8.1	11.9	10.9	8.2	11.0	7.3	7.6	u	u	7.5
Aged 14	9.5	10.7	10.1	10.1	18.0	10.8	11.3	10.8	17.2	(8.7)	(13.5)	11.9
Aged 15	14.5	14.3	13.9	13.9	17.4	13.5	13.5	12.5	13.2	9.2	10.8	10.7
Girls All ages	9.1	9.6	10.2	10.5	13.1	11.3	13.2	9.4	11.7	7.9	9.0	8.9
Aged 11-13	4.6	6.3	7.3	8.4	13.4	9.2	13.2	6.2	7.7	u	u	6.2
Aged 14	10.1	10.0	9.7	11.7	12.3	10.0	10.8	8.2	15.5	(8.9)	9.9	10.5
Aged 15	11.2	11.4	12.1	10.9	13.5	12.9	14.2	10.7	11.5	8.1	8.9	9.0

Source: Smoking, drinking and drug use among young people in England – 2016 - NHS Digital, 2017.

In 2003, a survey carried out by the BBC and the British Association of Accident and Emergency Medicine found that binge drinking on alcopops had resulted in the hospitalisation of children as young as six.

need2know

Drinking too much can make you feel invincible. Boys can get beaten up, mugged or attacked when under the influence. For girls, the biggest issue is usually their physical vulnerability. It's worth remembering the number one date rape drug is alcohol. According to the website Know Your Limits, one in three reported rapes happen when the victim has been drinking.

Drinking irresponsibly can place young people in risky situations, ranging from having a drink spiked and being raped, to getting arrested for throwing up in the street. Although the health issues are something certainly worth thinking about carefully, there's more to it than that. They can end up in legal trouble and be hit with an £80 fine for things like urinating or vomiting in the street, which are classed as anti-social behaviour.

Drunk girls are twice as likely to be sexually assaulted as boys. They also tend to find drinking large amounts more physically challenging, meaning they're more likely to throw up or pass out. Young people who are drunk are vulnerable to spiking as they're less aware of what's happening around them. And spiking drinks is an issue that's on the rise.

Watch where you're walking. Rapists are not confined to the heterosexual world but can be homosexual too. Do keep in mind that girls are not the only ones who can be taken advantage of while under the influence of alcohol. Drunk boys can – and do – get sexually assaulted.

What is also a fact is that 8 out of 10 pedestrians knocked down and killed on Friday or Saturday nights have been drinking. Accidents happen on the streets too, and when you're drunk, you wobble. You're not Superman. A number of pints can release the daredevil inside anyone. Many young people, especially teenage boys, can injure themselves by attempting stunts like climbing hoardings, scaffolding and fences while drunk.

Alcohol-related accidents and incidents, according to Know Your Limits, make up 70% of all A&E admissions between the hours of midnight and 5am. It's an unavoidable fact that drunk people have less control over their motor skills. You are not in control of your body, whether you believe it or not.

Drinking can lead to irresponsible sexual activity, leading to unwanted pregnancies and STIs. Both sexes need to think about the serious repercussions that can come from binge drinking. If both parties are somehow sober enough to consent (because drunk people are not in complete control of their bodies and thus cannot consent to sex), it's important that a condom is used. And keep in mind that a pint at the pub is not going to help with any special night you have planned with your sexual partner – "Brewer's Droop" is a real thing, and too much alcohol really will affect sexual performance.

The Dangerous Alcopop

Prettily packaged and sugary sweet like fruity fizzy drinks, the alcopop is, without a doubt, aimed specifically at a younger market. These days the alcopop is a far more sophisticated blend of taste, packaging and marketing. The teenage and underage drinking world is often dominated by alcopops. Drinks like Hooch and Two Dogs jumped on the scene when alcopops were launched in the UK drinks market around the mid 90s.

They paved the way for hundreds of imitators, as the sugary sharpness of this "alcoholic lemonade" was an instant success. In the early 2000s, Roxxoff – a vodka-based 'aphrodisiac' drink with a herbal libido enhancer – caused a fuss when it was released in the UK. Hilarious really, as too much booze definitely has the opposite effect on your sexual performance.

In 2013, however, it was reported by the BBC that teenagers were no longer drinking alcopops in such high numbers – opting, instead, for cheap beers and fruit-flavoured ciders. Rob Willock, editor of the Publican Morning Adviser, explained that "(Alcopops) enjoyed a classic product life cycle… When they burst on to the scene they were very popular. The moral panic that ensued did damage their prospects. They disappeared almost as quickly as they arrived." By now, it's believed that the impact of alcopops on young drinkers was greatly exaggerated even in the 1990s.

The Portman Group is a collective that was formed in 1989 by the UK's leading alcohol producers, as it says on their website 'to promote sensible drinking; to help prevent alcohol misuse; and to foster a balanced understanding of alcohol-related issues.' In its heyday, the alcopop faced considerable criticism by the Portman Group and other watchdogs. *(You can read more about the Portman Group and their values at their website,* **www.portmangroup.org.uk***.)*

Research carried out by sociologist Dr Alasdair Forsyth and his colleague has suggested that the main culprits in underage drinking are white cider and vodka. This is the opposite of what was announced by the media during the panic that surrounded alcopops, and as a result the continued consumption of these beverages has gone largely unnoted.

While alcopops' nice tastes and packaging did (and still do) appeal to young people, many of them are too expensive for teenagers to buy in large quantities. Low quality spirits and cider, meanwhile, can be bought in great amounts for a relatively low cost. Most young people are more interested in getting drunk for as little money as possible, than actually enjoying the taste of what it is they drink.

What Do I Do if My Child Is Drinking Underage?

It's an uncomfortable predicament to be in – being the parent of a teenager or young person, and worrying that they are drinking underage or binge drinking. How are you meant to deal with that problem?

Your first port of call should be talking to your child. Try and advise your child on how to say thanks no thanks without losing face, such as 'I don't like it', 'It's too high in calories' or 'It makes me sick'. Plan what you're going to say first and then open it like a conversation rather than a lecture. Most importantly, however, you should stay calm. This means calmly sitting down with them and discussing the positive aspects of a healthier lifestyle and the dangers of drinking alcohol, not just arguing and having a shouting match.

Make sure you're ready for any rebuttals or queries, and give your child the time to share their own opinions and ideas. Drink responsibly and make sure you're up-to-date on all the information relating to the dangers of alcohol, such as the physical effects, spiking and date rape and so on. Don't let them see you falling about drunk or drinking heavily all the time.

Teaching your child a sensible attitude needs to start with your own behaviour, as children often learn by example. It isn't good for you to drink large amounts of alcohol, and it isn't good for your children to see it. Above all, be realistic. If you know your stuff when it comes to alcohol, and follow your own advice, your offspring will be much more likely to respond positively.

Today's generation is no different to those that have come before: teenagers have always experimented with alcohol and other taboos. It's likely that you drank underage yourself.

Don't alienate your child. The last thing you want is for them to be afraid to call home – who knows what could happen then. Be sure they feel comfortable coming to you, and make sure they know that you'll always be there for them if something goes wrong, even when they've been drinking. Give them practical advice on how to avoid being mugged or spiked, and how to stay safe.

A Good Night Out

There are some golden rules to make sure you have a great night out that you'll actually remember when you go to the pub or club with your friends – whether you're old enough to drink or not.

Don't Go Out on an Empty Stomach

The rate at which alcohol enters your bloodstream will be slowed down if you've eaten recently. Eating before drinking will also help you feel less sick tomorrow morning.

Avoid Rounds

Drinking in rounds often means you have to drink faster to match everyone else's pace, and drink more as a result. Don't get sucked in!

Have a Soft Drink

Hydrating your body and laying off the alcohol will not only make you happier the next morning, it'll improve your night out in the first place. Try alternating alcoholic drinks with non-alcoholic drinks. This is a great way to lessen your intake without feeling left out. You'll be much better at dancing, and will have way more energy!

> Many young people find themselves being nagged to join in with their friends or drinking buddies. Don't let them get under your skin.

Ignore Peer Pressure

Real mates shouldn't be giving you a hard time, but if you feel there are those that can't accept you want to drink less, you could always pull the old antibiotics story, or say you're driving. Many young people find themselves being nagged to join in with their friends or drinking buddies. Don't let them get under your skin.

Don't Touch the Strong Stuff

You'll have a worse hangover and get much more drunk if you drink strong continental beers like Kronenbourg or Stella, however great the idea seems at the time. These beers can sometimes contain a whole unit more than weaker drinks.

Watch What You're Drinking

Don't line your drinks up, keep track of your intake. Make sure you have plenty of mixers too. Try to opt for the single shot rather than the double, or the smaller of the wine glasses. Shots can creep up and knock you out from behind, so try to keep these to a minimum.

Know How You're Getting Home

Make sure you know how you're getting home before you start out. Don't get into a car if the driver has been drinking, don't use unlicensed taxis, don't accept a lift from a stranger and don't walk home alone. This may all sound obvious, but a lot of people completely ignore this advice when they've had too much to drink.

Water before Bed

This tip works miracles. You'll really thank yourself when you wake up if you have a nice big glass of water before you head to bed (and take one with you)!

Summing Up

- Underage drinking is still a very big problem.

- Many young people find it hard to stay in control of how much they drink. They can end up getting in trouble as a result.

- Saying "no thanks" when surrounded by other people who are drinking can be very difficult.

- Skipping a drink or two could very well save your life, and either way you'll thank yourself in the morning.

- Be sure to listen to your child and learn about their thoughts and experiences.

- Don't lecture!

- If your child is the one drinking, communication is key.

- Very young children are being admitted to hospital with alcohol-related troubles and the rise of binge drinking amongst teenagers and young people is alarming.

5

What Does Alcoholism Do to Your Body?

The Effects of Alcohol

Long term drinking can lead to high blood pressure, heart disease, breast cancer, liver failure and strokes. But what actually happens to the body when you drink?

Excessive drinking is bad for you – everyone knows that. It's not a glamorous disease to have. As a close-up example of the effects of drinking, let's take a look at what happens in your body on a big night out.

Getting the First Round at the Pub

Your body feels great after the first drink of the night. It produces a lovely effect as alcohol begins to enter your bloodstream. Alcohol affecting your CNS (central nervous system) is what creates this feeling. The early stages of intoxication during the first few hours of drinking begin to interfere with all of the bodily functions that your CNS controls – things like your speech and senses.

You might speak louder, laugh a lot, talk to people more effusively, and dance with gay abandon! People drinking will begin to lose their inhibitions as the alcohol begins to affect their frontal cortex, the area of the brain that controls behaviour. Alcohol is also a diuretic, which makes you urinate too much, leading to dehydration and that inevitable 'morning after' feeling.

It becomes increasingly difficult to stand still, walk in a straight line or speak clearly, as further drinking continues to affect the functionality of the CNS.

A Good Few Down the Line

Your ability to feel the sensation of pain will become diminished as time goes on and the drinking continues. Other effects will also become more intense: you have blurred vision, your senses are picking up on fewer signals, and you're sweating more than usual. You'll also get to the stage now where you might be emotional, and this can lead to aggression or perhaps being tearful.

Your liver has to process the alcohol, if your body is unable to store it. You're heading straight for hangover city now: the liver can only process one unit of alcohol per hour, so if you're drinking more than this and not drinking plenty of water at the same time, you're going to be pretty dehydrated. Being dehydrated means the kidneys have had to draw water from the other organs and parts of the body, just to flush the alcohol through.

Another Few Drinks

By now, you're probably staggering about. The alcohol is slowing down your reaction time, and messing with your coordination. If you continue drinking, you're going to be really ill. It's time to call it a night.

> By now, you're probably staggering about. The alcohol is slowing down your reaction time, and messing with your coordination. If you continue drinking, you're going to be really ill. It's time to call it a night.

Crashing Out

You decide to hit the hay as you've had too much to drink and are feeling tired and emotional. Your body isn't letting you sleep, though! Alcohol affects your sleep rhythms and patterns, as well as making you snore and disturbing your sleep (and whoever's fortunate enough to share a room with you) by relaxing your throat muscles. You're likely to feel pretty ill, as your body is completely dehydrated. It's unlikely you'll wake up feeling refreshed.

Coming To

When you wake up, you feel lethargic and unsteady as your glucose levels are at rock bottom. You feel pretty wretched! People crave high carbohydrate snacks the morning after, and this is because of the sugar crash. Aside from this, alcohol irritates the stomach, which can lead to retching and heartburn, and affects the bowel, causing diarrhoea.

You're also exhausted from a late night combined with too little sleep, and the dehydration has given you a headache. Imagine putting your body through that trauma every day of your life.

The Morning After

You'll definitely be over the limit the next morning if you've had too much to drink the night before, as the liver can only deal with a maximum of two units per hour.

Lightheadedness, extreme thirstiness and muscle cramps can all be issues the morning after the night before, as alcohol uses up the minerals and vitamins in the body, especially potassium. In addition to this, dehydration is going to make your body ache all over, especially your head. Your body is unable to handle all of the toxins it has produced.

In a bid to stave off the results of yesterday's excess, a person who is alcohol dependent or addicted will likely reach for another drink to deal with the pain – the 'hair of the dog that bit you'.

Excessive drinking can quickly spiral out of control and do real physical and social damage. Just read the case study below.

Case Study: Beth

Rather than a traditional alcoholic, Beth was a classic binge drinker. She gave up drinking at the beginning of 2018 and is attending AA meetings. She has an important job as a HR consultant, but suffers badly from compulsive disorders, shyness and anxiety. So to combat this feeling of fear, Beth often relied on alcohol to take her nerves away.

"Parties are the absolute worst, they fill me with complete terror. It's completely out of my control in a very strange way. You know what? It's weird. I have a really responsible job that I love and am really good at. I spend all day dealing with people's work issues, making decisions, planning events and talking to people face to face.

"What I find really hard to deal with, though, is social situations – like a night out with a group of friends. I always just feel like I'd rather climb on the sofa under a duvet than go out. I spend hours feeling unbearably anxious, butterflies in my stomach. No matter what I do, I can't reason with myself over this. I know it's just my friends, and I love seeing them, but I just can't get past the anxiety."

Beth began from a very early age to use alcohol as a prop to handle nights out, finding that it could take the edge off her fears. Beth found that her friends ran out of patience with her and she was invited out less and less. She confesses:

"As soon as my inhibitions are removed, so is any moderation, and before I know it, I'm absolutely legless and being a complete idiot. I can't stop once I've started, that's the issue. I'm incapable of taking it easy, even when alcohol makes me feel more relaxed. I tend to start drinking before I leave my house, so by the time I get to the event I'm way ahead of everyone else. And still, I can't stop. That just isn't how it works. I can get really bloody annoying, it's like flicking a switch. One minute I'm nice, normal Beth. The next, I've had two or three glasses of dry white and am a drunken idiot with a mental age of about five.

"Going out and getting drunk together was a normal thing to do a few years back, when we were all a little younger. I think I saw those days as being fun you know, a bit edgy, like it was hilarious to get legless every day of the weekend and do stupid things. We used to go out clubbing and stuff, start our big Friday night out in the bar. The whole "mad night out" plan has happened less and less as we've got older. Some of us have children now, and some are married or own businesses.

"Whatever we did, though, I would continue to drink myself stupid. If I went to someone's house for dinner, I wouldn't just take one bottle of wine, I'd take three, and then drink at least that much or more. My mates would be putting me in cabs to send me home or whatever, even if we were just meant to be going out for dinner or a couple of drinks.

"I'd ring up and apologise sometimes and I could feel that they were annoyed with me. Every time, I was the one who got the most out of it. I completely ruined loads of weekends, holidays, weekends away, even Christmases and New Year's Eves, just because I'd be drunk and spoiling it for everyone else. The next day, I'd always wake up feeling completely mortified.

"Unless I had anything particular to do I would then get up and start drinking again, just so I didn't have to think about it."

The feelings of embarrassment and remorse would often lead Beth to drink over a period of days too, something that her boyfriend struggled to deal with.

"I would hear about fun nights that others had had, but nobody would have asked me. I think people stopped asking me along because I just kept ruining their night out. I always hated knowing that I'd been left out, even though I knew the idea of going out filled me with fear.

"I'd know in the back of my mind something was wrong as soon as I woke up, I just felt really weird. And I just wanted to pull the duvet over my head and die when I eventually remembered what I'd done the night before. Another lost weekend. To be honest, even if I had something important to do I often just started drinking at that point.

"I didn't realise it at the time, but I was definitely being a right pain in the neck. All the drinking really did was drive my boyfriend away.

When she realised she was dangerously close to losing everything, Beth decided it was time to give up drinking. She quickly discovered that even though she was unable to control herself when she started drinking, she could quite easily just not start drinking in the first place. So Beth quit, lucky enough to be one of those for whom the physical addiction is not the main issue. She wasn't a "classic" alcoholic. Beth explains:

"I always found it weirdly easy to go back to normal as soon as Monday morning came. No problem, just like anyone else. Every day during the week, I'd be able to get up and go to work without taking a drink all day. I was even able to have a single glass of wine with dinner in the evening. But I'd be off when Friday night rolled around. I still don't know what happened, but one Sunday morning I woke up somewhere I'd never been before with no idea how I got there. My clothes were torn and covered in sick, and my bag was missing. I knew then I had to take control of this before it killed me or ruined my life. My boyfriend was really sick of this rollercoaster, and I know I was going to lose him. I was going to ruin his life, and the lives of everyone who cared about me."

At the moment, Beth is concentrating on taking control. Interestingly, those feelings of fear and anxiety when faced with social situations have diminished greatly since quitting, something she wasn't expecting. She's hopeful that someday she'll be able to relax and share one glass of wine with her friends, to practice moderation.

"It's been great actually. It's really loads easier than I thought. My anxiety is much better now, and not just when it comes to going out. My outlook on life has changed a lot too. I think the booze was making it worse, and perhaps part of the fear was knowing I was going to go out and make an idiot of myself. I didn't think I'd be able to go out without drinking, because I always dreaded it and had to drink to deal with the fear.

"But it's not like that. It's completely fine now. I don't stay long, not yet. I'm able to go to a pub or bar and just have a nice cup of coffee. Alcohol is still a temptation if I stay out too long. I can still have a really nice time sober. I go to friends' houses for dinner now and just drink juice. My friends were completely fed up with my drinking before, so they're all really pleased I've done this. Everyone has kind of said "thank god". Overall, it's been really great, if a little strange.

"I've lost loads of weight, and feel much more clear headed and optimistic. I thought I wasn't an alcoholic so these meetings wouldn't apply to me, but actually it's not just about that. Right now, AA meetings are really helping me. I wanted to do all this on my own, but my boyfriend encouraged me to go. Eventually, I decided I may as well give it a go. I went along to a meeting after I spoke to someone from the AA who was really dead on. Talking to other people who know what I'm on about has been great."

All names in case studies are changed to protect the speaker's identity.

How Much Is Too Much?

While previous guidelines stated different drinking limits for men and women, the Department of Health's current guidelines state a single limit for men and women. This is because although women are at greater risk of long-term health harm, men have a higher risk of immediate harm and it's believed these points balance each other out. The new guideline is weekly rather than daily, as this applies more appropriately to the ways in which people drink today.

The current recommendation for both men and women is to keep your alcohol intake below 14 units per week. Don't save units for bingeing though, as this places extra pressure on your system, and do at least one alcohol free day a week – give your poor liver a chance to recover. For those who drink amounts on the higher end of this limit, it's recommended that the drinking is spread over three or more days.

The Department of Health have suggested the following quantities as a guideline for what makes up a unit:

One 275ml bottle of an alcopop (ABV 5.5%)	=	approx 1.5 units
One pint of strong lager (ABV 5%)	=	3 units
A single measure of spirits (ABV 37.5%)	=	1 unit
Half a pint of average-strength lager (4%)	=	1 unit
Two thirds of a 125ml glass of average-strength (12%) wine	=	1 unit

How Does Drinking Affect Your Body?

The damage isn't just repaired once the hangover is gone, however much it might feel like it. Your body will really start to be affected if you drink excessively over a long period of time.

Putting on Weight

Weight increase is a common issue, because there are a lot of calories in alcohol. You might also eat more than is necessary at home of the wrong kind of food. And the curry house or chipper can be really tempting on a night out – anyone drinking a large amount will often pick up poor eating habits.

Skin Complaints

Alcohol also dilates your capillaries, the tiny veins just under the surface of your skin, which can break, leading to unsightly redness and broken veins on the face. Your skin is likely to become dull and dry – being dehydrated all the time can have a really negative effect. It's not a great look.

Alcohol also dilates your capillaries, the tiny veins just under the surface of your skin, which can break, leading to unsightly redness and broken veins on the face.

The Eyes Have It

Bloodshot eyes are a common side effect of drinking too much. The blood vessels in your eyes can become damaged by alcohol, just like the capillaries in your face.

Smell Something?

Your poor liver struggles to process all the alcohol and your body tries to help out by excreting it through sweat, urine and of course, your breath. That morning after smell is never pleasant.

Battered Body

Cuts, bruises, broken bones and scars are all part of the pattern. Violence and clumsiness are common issues for big drinkers.

What Happens in the Long Run?

If you know you have a drink problem, read this carefully. It's bad for you to drink excessively over a long period of time. If you've read this far into the book, you'll know that by now. Any of the following conditions can be caused or aggravated by drinking. The damage can be far worse than a nasty hangover.

- Liver cancer, or cirrhosis of the liver.
- Cardiomyopathy (damage to heart muscle).
- Unhealthy weight gain.
- Stroke (brain haemorrhage).
- Liver disease, high blood pressure, diabetes, stress.
- Inflamed pancreas (pancreatitis).
- Alcohol poisoning (which can be fatal).
- Stomach problems such as ulcers.
- Sexual difficulties, including impotence.
- Coronary heart disease.
- Infertility.

- High blood pressure.
- Breast cancer.

Remember, these physical effects aren't even all you have to worry about. The following mental health issues are common in people who drink a lot:

- Unhappiness and lack of motivation.
- Altered personality.
- Reduced libido.
- "Seeing things".
- Mood swings.
- Memory loss.
- Dementia and mental impairments.
- Poor concentration.
- Suicidal feelings.

What to Do in an Emergency

If you are with someone you know has been drinking heavily, and the symptoms include vomiting, sweating, laboured or shallow breathing or unconsciousness, you need to act. Death, coma and unconsciousness are all very real risks if you drink too much at once. When this happens, and those around the person are also drunk, these emergencies are rarely handled properly. It's one of the least recognised emergencies.

Allowing them to lie on their back can mean vomit could choke them. Place the victim in the recovery position before you do anything else. This basically means lying the person on their side – look it up now if you don't know what this should look like. Make sure you can hear them breathing and check their pulse. The next thing you need to do is ring for help. Stay with the person and call an ambulance. Stay calm and wait for help.

The victim is at risk of suffocation if they vomit, so try to make sure their airways are clear at all times.

Summing Up

- Over a long period of time and/or in large doses, alcohol can be really bad for you.

- The liver has a way of mending and regenerating itself, so stopping drinking really can make a huge difference to your current and future health.

- The prognosis isn't good for people who drink for a long time.

- Heart disease, cancer, liver disease and all those real bad guys are all there for the alcohol abuser.

- Learning to cope with an emergency could help save someone's life, but it's also important, whether you're an alcoholic or living with someone with a drink problem, to know what alcohol does to your body.

6

Pregnancy and Drinking

Women who drink heavily and repeatedly throughout their pregnancy are risking damaging their babies and the effects will last a lifetime. Overall, the effects can be quite devastating, with the general impression being of a person who is not drastically unwell, but just not functioning properly on most or many levels. In the late 70s, the first case of Foetal Alcohol Syndrome (FAS) was diagnosed based on estimates from the World Health Organisation.

The odd glass of wine during pregnancy isn't usually going to have a drastic effect, but according to Dr Raja Mukherjee, a psychiatrist specialising in FAS, even moderate amounts can have an effect. The condition is now believed to affect as many as 450,000 people living in Britain. Birth defects are common, as are physical abnormalities such as skeletal weakness or neurological damage. Their mental age will be affected and they will have trouble developing emotionally. Memory can be affected too, with the sufferer having problems retaining information or losing short term memory.

Avoiding alcohol entirely during pregnancy is the only way you can guarantee your child won't be born with FAS.

The Damage

Infants born with foetal alcohol syndrome are often born premature and are highly likely to be underweight.

As a general rule, the extent of the damage will be determined by how much the mother drank during pregnancy.

With so many children being increasingly diagnosed with Attention Deficit Disorder, Susan Fleisher of the National Association on Foetal Alcohol Syndrome has raised a possibility that FAS could be the reason for the rise. Many children with foetal alcohol syndrome will feel isolated as they grow up, and will have trouble engaging with their peers.

Infants born with foetal alcohol syndrome are often born premature and are highly likely to be underweight.

Ostracisation is common, and these children stand a very high chance of being bullied at school. Weaker, smaller bones can make physical development another challenge for children with FAS.

Life, as a whole, can become unnecessarily difficult.

Susan Fleisher explains:

"We are seeing children at nursery with attention deficit disorder who could be the products of mothers who had a binge drink three years earlier, before they knew they were pregnant."

It's an interesting theory that definitely gives pause for thought. Fleisher also believes that binge drinking during pregnancy could also be the cause for the rising levels of crime among older children. These children are being directly affected by the rise of binge drinking among young women.

What Effect Does Alcohol Have on a Foetus

Permanent damage can occur when a pregnant mother drinks alcohol. A lot depends on physical and genetic makeup. In severe cases, symptoms include underweight babies; slow growth rate; deformed ears; small eyes; slow development of the optic nerve and short-sightedness; skeletal defects; heart damage; a small head; a thin upper lip and small teeth and mental retardation.

The alcohol molecules are small enough that they can pass easily through the placenta, killing off the foetus' nerve endings and the connections between their brain cells. Difficulty with social and emotional relationships can be an issue for children with less severe cases of Foetal Alcohol Spectrum Disorder. They may also have symptoms like hyperactivity, poor short-term memory, poor coordination, difficulty understanding abstract concepts, lower IQ and immature behaviour.

In some cases, a mother consuming alcohol will have truly devastating effects on their unborn child. In other cases, the foetus will cope with the alcohol relatively well. The extent of the damage can also be affected by the stage of the pregnancy at which the mother consumed alcohol, with the earlier stages being the most vulnerable. But whenever drinking takes place, it can have a detrimental effect.

The mother's overall health and well-being also plays a role.

The foetus' skeleton and face are developing in the early stages of pregnancy, so drinking at this point is most likely to lead to physical deformities. Brain damage, issues with the nervous system and low IQ are more likely to occur when the mother drinks in the later stages of pregnancy, as this is when these parts are developing.

Summing Up

- It can be tempting to continue drinking despite your pregnancy, as you may feel left out of social engagements without alcohol. If you have an alcohol addiction, it will be especially difficult to stop drinking, but you have to do it for the health of you and your unborn child.

- You are carrying what will soon turn into another human being. Drinking now will not only threaten your life and health, but the future life of the person inside you.

- Whether it's you or your partner that has the drinking problem, you should seek medical help as soon as possible. Try contacting your GP.

- It's vital that you take care of yourself during pregnancy, and even if you lapse back afterwards, at least you can feel more positive that you have given the baby a better head start.

- People with FAS have long term problems and can be completely dysfunctional, leading to unhappy and difficult lives.

- Getting help for a drink problem is always going to be a good idea, but it's even more important when pregnant.

7

Dealing with the Reality

Do I Have a Problem?

It will never be easy to live with someone who is alcohol dependant, or to be alcohol dependant yourself. Partners and children often look to themselves and their own behaviour to try to identify a source for it all, wondering perhaps if they behaved differently, would the problem go away. Surely the drinker can see the damage they're doing?

Home can become a stressful place to be – disordered, complicated, often filled with arguments. This is often particularly upsetting for children if one or both of their parents have a drinking problem, as they will constantly be comparing their life to the happy, average lives of their friends. It's impossible to see a good reason for all the turmoil, so it's very difficult to come to terms with all of this. It's so hard to see why else all of this could be happening, so it's easy for the "why me?" question to work its way into their line of thought.

Nothing you have done could possibly have caused this, though it's hard to realise that. This is not your fault. You will also never be able to make someone who is addicted to or dependant on alcohol change their ways. It absolutely has to come from the addict. "Why me?" is just as potent a question for them, and they will struggle to understand what makes them like this. You can support them once they decide to change, but ultimately it has to be their decision.

It's equally hard to understand why this has happened to you if you're the one who has realised that you have an addiction.

Social Embarrassment

A glass of wine at dinner, champagne at a wedding, a few too many at a party – all of these things are acceptable social variables, but dealing with continuous excessive drinking is not okay. After all, who wants someone as volatile as the alcoholic at the dinner table? It is widely understood that it's a fun, communal thing to drink socially. The fun ends when the drinking leads to mortification for everyone else and guilt for the drinker.

Public appearances can be a minefield, with the alcoholic pretty much hell bent on simply drinking as much as they can to get through it, or possibly even turning up drunk. The behaviour that goes with continuous excessive drinking can cause embarrassment to the drinker and everyone around them. However, no matter how awful their behaviour might have been, and how embarrassing it has been for all concerned, one of the major factors the alcoholic faces when confronting their problem is the stigma of being labelled as someone with a "drink problem".

Just think of the story in Beth's Case Study. Over time, the individual is likely to receive fewer and fewer social invitations to dinners and get-togethers, as neighbours and loved ones can find their drinking a bit much to deal with. They can never know if they can rely on the drinker to behave themselves or not. Accidentally abetting and assisting their loved one's addiction, the family of an alcoholic will often try to cover up or underplay the problem in a bid to maintain some appearance of respectability, or at least normality.

Messes are explained away or tidied up, excuses and lies are invented. Nobody wants people to know their relative has this sort of problem. It can be incredibly difficult to openly admit that you or a loved one has an alcohol addiction, with one of the main feelings associated with alcohol dependence being a sense of shame and loneliness.

Accepting There Is Something Wrong

According to Prochaska and DiClemente, the path that the recovering alcoholic will usually tread is broken down into five recognisable stages; Pre-contemplation, Contemplation, Preparation, Action and Maintenance. The alcoholic is very often the last person to admit that there is a problem. Some alcoholics will never be able to accept that this is the case, and it's very sad when this happens.

Some people who are dependent on alcohol will end up never dealing with the problem, continuing to live with the addiction without coming to terms with it.

If, or when, the alcoholic in your life does come to discover they have a problem, the following stages are likely to occur.

Pre-Contemplation

The alcoholic will reject any suggestion that there is a problem, usually being angry and defensive about it. They will try to refute any kind of suggestion that they need help and their life will be chaotic. Denial is still strong at this stage in the process. They're likely to seek out situations where drinking is acceptable, or drinking buddies who will condone and conceal the amount they drink. Any suggestions of treatment will be thrown out.

Contemplating

The drinker is faced with the undeniable fact that they have a problem, usually only after things have become really bad. This is often a real sock in the jaw, with the alcohol dependant slowly coming to the realisation that things have to change, and change for good. It's really hard for them to face up to this. Often this requires a crisis of some form. There will be an overwhelming sense of the enormity of what's happened and happening, and anxiety or depression may become a problem.

Some people who are dependent on alcohol will end up never dealing with the problem, continuing to live with the addiction without coming to terms with it.

Preparation

Severe alcoholism is going to cause intense physical reaction and, for all, some level of detox is needed. The person with the problem will begin to consider the different ways of moving forward at preparation stage. Most will need addiction counselling and support, and other forms of therapy such as marital or family counselling will be needed to help repair any damage done to loved ones around. It can be really daunting, depending on the severity of the problem, but this is a positive stage overall. Medication for withdrawal may be necessary, and some will even require in-patient care.

Taking Action

This is where the alcohol begins to take active steps towards their recovery. It's not unusual for action to be short-lived or followed soon after by relapse, so the support of family and friends is vital for the success of this stage. Finding something that makes a permanent difference can take a few tries.

Maintenance

In order to stay on the right path, the recovered alcoholic needs to stay alert to potential areas of temptation, such as going out with old drinking partners, having booze around the house, stressful situations that would normally have them reaching for the bottle and so on. However much a person thinks they have recovered, it's vital that they continue with this final, ongoing stage. Having the empathy and support of those who have been through something similar can make a massive difference, so support groups like Alcoholics Anonymous can be invaluable for this lengthy and sometimes never-ending stage.

Summing Up

- There is always hope.

- It is never easy to admit your problem to relatives, colleagues or friends, but those that care about you will support you and knowing that the problem is finally being addressed often provides some relief. The "drinker" or "ex-drinker" label isn't an appealing prospect, but the other option is to continue with an addiction that can eventually kill you.

- The best plan is to take things one day at a time, and to remain realistic but optimistic.

- The hardest part is making the decision to change.

- Anyone who has reached that decision can feel very proud of themselves straightaway.

- The path to recovery is never easy, and relapses often happen.

- If it's you who has come to this realisation, you can give yourself a massive pat on the back; you're about to make a fantastic change.

- Once an alcoholic has made a decision to get help and has put this into action, there is a good chance things will work out okay.

8

Support for Kids

Children of Alcoholics

Anyone who has lived with an alcoholic mother or father will know what a rollercoaster home life can become. It's also a tragic fact that alcohol contributes heavily to the occurrence of abuse, both sexual and physical. Children who have grown up with alcoholic parents tend to bear fundamental emotional and behavioural scars, according to a 2006 report by the UK addiction specialists, Priority Healthcare.

Research into previous studies undertaken as part of the Priory report discovered that 70% of those children with alcohol abuse in their homes went on to develop compulsive behaviour themselves, whether it might be addictions to alcohol, drugs, gambling, sex or even food – and about half of them ended up marrying or living with alcoholics or alcohol abusers when they grew up.

While this may seem obvious to some readers, others may not realise the damage they or someone else could be doing to the children in their lives. Many children are made to live with chaos, guilt, confusion and arguments. Many people with drinking problems seek to pin the blame for their problem on someone else, and often it is the children who are made to shoulder that blame.

According to the study, 55% of domestic violence happened in alcoholic homes and 90% of child abuse cases involved alcohol abuse. Existing figures on abuse, alcohol and crime, as well as consultation with priority healthcare therapists and doctors, were used to compile the 2006 report. It was found that girls in alcohol-abusing homes were up to four times more likely to experience sexual abuse.

While this is not, of course, a foregone conclusion and should never be seen as such, the children of people who abused alcohol were found to be four times more likely to develop a drinking problem in the future. This comes down to a combination of learnt behaviour and genetics. The report also discovered that they found it difficult to develop strong personal relationships.

There are three main ways a child is likely to react to alcoholism, according to the report. Some children will use their background to their advantage by becoming stronger, some will develop withdrawn, shy personalities and others will end up living in denial. The report clarifies, however, that no matter how composed a child may appear on the outside, this is simply their outward appearance: "Their feelings about themselves are the opposite of the serene image they present – they generally feel insecure, inadequate, dull, unsuccessful, vulnerable and anxious."

So if you are one of those children who have a parent suffering from this condition, please don't feel alone. It's estimated that the general average for people living with this damaging condition is around 1 in 20 – possibly the most shocking finding from the study. There's a lot of help available to all concerned, as this issue is much more common than many would believe.

> Many people with drinking problems seek to pin the blame for their problem on someone else, and often it is the children who are made to shoulder that blame.

Does Your Parent Have a Drinking Problem?

If there is someone with an alcohol problem in your family, it affects every single member. You probably won't want to have your mates round for fear of embarrassment and there's every chance that you're getting the blame for all of this, and that it's your fault mum or dad drinks. Coming home becomes a journey of fear – what is waiting for you when you get back?

Or you might simply feel saddened watching someone you love wasting their life, focused on alcohol and seemingly not much else.

Alcohol addiction is a family issue. This is a very accurate description, so you're likely to hear it a lot in circles that know about the disease. The whole household suffers when the person with the addiction is having a bad time, and the whole household is happy when things are good. Listening in bed for the sound of violence or fighting can make night times frightening.

If you fear for your own safety from abuse or violence, things can be even scarier.

Nobody else seems to bother with things like food or cleaning, so you may well find yourself assuming responsibility in the house. Who will wash your school uniform or cook the dinner if you don't?

Living like this isn't very much fun.

You're Not Alone

Studies conducted by the National Association for Children of Alcoholics have shown that there are close to a million people under the age of 18 in the UK living with parents who have an alcohol problem. You are definitely not alone, however tough it is to live with someone with an alcohol problem. Don't let it hold you back.

- You mustn't allow yourself to feel like you have to hide this problem from the world, or that this is your fault somehow.

- The decision to stop drinking has to come from the person with the problem. They need help, but do keep in mind that you can't make them stop drinking or change their life for them.

- Try not to feel embarrassed or ashamed about the person who is an alcoholic – alcoholism is a disease and it's absolutely not your fault.

A Problem Shared Is a Problem Halved

It's really common for children and teenagers to feel like they have to keep the problem to themselves if they find themselves in this situation. Choosing to keep a low profile, they avoid discussing the situation with anyone else. Talking to someone is the best thing you can do for yourself. It could be a teacher you trust at school or college, a friend's mum or dad, a family friend or another relative.

You may well find that the person you talk to will be able to help, and at the very least it will feel like a massive relief to let out all your pent-up concerns. They may be able to offer you somewhere to hang out when you need a bit of quiet, security or peace. They can offer you practical support, like a spare bed, or maybe just some understanding and guidance to give you strength.

Get out more, try to enjoy life and immerse yourself in doing things that will make you feel better about yourself and cheer you up. Getting involved in fun extracurricular activities outside of home and school is another way to help you deal with the problems at home. Whatever anyone says at home, you have great potential and it's important that you act on it.

Tips for an Easier Life

Hiding drink or pouring it away won't work if you're trying to stop the drinking. But there are ways to detach yourself from the drinking part, and still love that person for who they are, aside from the drinking. If you want to make life easier at home, your best bet is to just try and avoid arguments or tension when your parents have been drinking.

The person with the alcohol problem loves you, but they are making life hard for you. Understand that it's okay (and in fact very common) to feel both love and hate for the person in question. You're going to be upset and angry a lot of the time, so conflicting emotions are completely normal for people in your situation. Don't beat yourself up about it. It may be easier to come at home if you attend a support group, as they can be the key in coming to understand and accept difficult situations.

Concerned for a Child in Your Life?

You could be seriously worried about physical or sexual abuse going on in the home and really want to help, but don't know how to. How you proceed with this will depend very much on who you are and who you are worried about. You may want to try and help in some way if you know a family with an alcohol problem that could potentially be causing harm to a child or teenager.

Be prepared for initial rejection though – it's very normal for children in this situation to be in denial or embarrassed. Maybe you can have a chat with the young people if you're a friend of the family, relative or teacher, and the child is old enough to understand what you have to say. Let them know that you are there, and ask gently about any issues they may be facing.

Don't delay though, and be strong about it. If you're willing to help in any way you can, make sure they know that you're available to help them. Even if they reject you initially, they may well come around in time.

If the children involved are infants, though, or if you don't know the family well enough, it can be trickier. There are a number of groups you could try talking to if this is the case. For example, the National Association for Children of Alcoholics is a great place to start. You can call them on 0800 358 3456, or check out their website **www.nacoa.org.uk**. Regardless of how close your relationship might be with the family, the appropriate authorities will need to be contacted as soon as possible if the children concerned are in any real danger.

Whoever the perpetrator is, it's essential that all children are protected from harm and abuse. Imagine if you did nothing and the worst happened. You may feel like you're betraying someone, but you may well be saving a life.

Children's Support Options

It's true to say that you can't make your parent or carer stop drinking – that has to come from them. You might feel pretty powerless if you're the child of someone with a drinking problem. But you're not powerless. We've already talked about family, friends or teachers who could be the shoulder you need, but there are other options too. There are things you can do that will help you deal with the unhappiness and confusion of your situation.

Al-Anon runs a support group called Alateen, which was set up specifically for the children and teenagers of people who abuse alcohol. This helps the younger members of families with alcohol problems and friends of alcoholics. An Alateen group, or something similar, may well exist in your area.

If you need to talk, you can just pick up the phone. A freephone helpline (0800 358 3456) is run by the National Association for Children of Alcoholics (**www.nacoa.org.uk**), which we have already mentioned. This freephone number is for use by children and teenagers of all ages, with almost a quarter of the calls received coming from seven-year-olds.

There are people who can help you. For more resources, check out the help list at the back of this book.

It's true to say that you can't make your parent or carer stop drinking – that has to come from them. You might feel pretty powerless if you're the child of someone with a drinking problem. But you're not powerless.

Summing Up

- Life can sometimes become unbearable for the children of one or more parents with alcohol addictions.

- Try to find interests outside the home that you can enjoy, and stay calm. Always remember that none of this is your fault.

- You may well be reading this book as a parent with a drinking problem. If this is the case, try to understand that alcohol abuse will damage your child and it's time to make a change.

- Stepping in before alcoholism ruins a child's life is very important.

- If it's someone else's children you're worried about as you read this, don't delay in seeking advice.

- Things change and you may find that your mum or dad makes a change for the better, or perhaps it's simply the time when you can move out that you will be looking forward to, but above all, find someone you can talk to.

- Eventually of course you will be old enough to leave it all behind, but there are ways to cope whilst you have no choice but to remain.

9

Fixing Things

Making the Decision

Making the decision to quit the booze is not something anyone else can do for a person who is alcohol dependent; the only person who can make that decision is them. Once the decision has been made, the next step is to form some kind of plan; work out whether you'll need help with the physical effects of withdrawal; plan how your counselling or support strategy will work and put in place incentives and deterrents to help avoid falling off the wagon as time progresses.

So if it's you giving up, be aware of that. On your way down the road to recovery, the first and most important step you'll have to take is deciding it's time to give up alcohol. It's important to recognise just how hard making this choice is – it may well be the most difficult thing you'll ever have to do.

Inevitably, all the people around the person with the problem will need to get involved once the decision has been made. The rest of the journey isn't going to be easy, and you'll need help. Choosing to change may be the hardest part, but that doesn't mean the other steps won't be difficult too.

I Want to Stop Drinking

Cold Turkey

Withdrawal symptoms can potentially make going cold turkey quite dangerous for someone who is heavily dependent on alcohol. So start to look into options for medical support and ensure aftercare is in place once the severe withdrawal symptoms have passed. If you think you can safely come off drinking at home, start to make plans for that.

Even without the medical factor, it's a very difficult way of going about things. It may well be some time before you can feel fully healthy, as years of drinking will have taken their toll on your body. Take time off work for this – if you're employed, you're not going to be at your best for a few days.

Try making it really hard for yourself to buy alcohol by putting someone else in charge of your cash and cards, and remove all the alcohol from your house to avoid temptation. It'll rise again, believe me, and you'll be back to square one. Instead, stock up on fruit juices and other soft drinks to keep your sugar levels up – alcohol tends to have a very high sugar content, so you may well feel the effects of low blood sugar when you stop taking it.

Keeping your sugars up should also help with symptoms like shakiness and low mood.

> Try making it really hard for yourself to buy alcohol by putting someone else in charge of your cash and cards, and remove all the alcohol from your house to avoid temptation.

Giving Up Gradually

Many people find it easier to cut down their drinking before giving it up entirely, so it can be good to take a less severe approach. The best way to use this method is to schedule a clear strategy and timeline, setting goals for how much to reduce by for certain dates and sticking to it. It's easy for the quantity to start creeping up again if not managed and monitored carefully, but done right this method will reduce your level of physical reliance on alcohol.

Don't ever forget your ultimate goal is to give up completely. Be sure to avoid the trap of thinking it's alright to keep drinking if you do it in moderation. Giving yourself a time limit for the period of reduction can be a good way to do this. Make sure you stick to your goals, and keep in mind that this period of moderate drinking is only temporary.

Telling Friends and Family

Explain to your friends and family what you are doing and ask for their help.

Being under the influence of alcohol on a regular and frequent basis will have clouded your judgement to a greater or lesser degree, but it's not uncommon for alcohol abusers to be unaware of the impact that they are having on those around them.

Many people worry about being left open to judgement from family and friends if they "go public" about their drinking problem. Admitting to a drinking problem can even feel embarrassing to some people. Keep in mind, however, that most people in your life will be thrilled that you're finally dealing with the problem, as they will already have noticed that your drinking had become an issue.

You may be surprised when you discover just how many people have been affected by – and concerned about – your alcohol consumption. You may well have an understanding of the pressure it's put on your immediate family, but it's likely to have reached even further than that.

Going it alone will be incredibly difficult, so having the support of your friends and family at this time is really important.

What's Going to Happen?

Anyone who is alcohol dependent will experience some unpleasantness – those with milder addictions will have less severe symptoms of course, but heavy or very long term alcohol abuse, going cold turkey can be pretty rough. Withdrawal symptoms are the first main issue you'll need to take into account when you quit drinking. The following symptoms may occur:

Withdrawal Symptoms

Moderate and Mild Symptoms:

- Feeling anxious, tense or shaky.
- Vomiting or feeling queasy.
- Feeling depressed.
- Reduced concentration.

- Not feeling hungry.

- Bad dreams.

- Tiredness and/or insomnia.

- Being irritable or overemotional.

- Headaches, sweating, having palpitations.

If you're a heavy user, you're going to need medical help, so make sure you put that in place before starting – you're far better off somewhere where there are qualified medics to help you and it could be dangerous to do this at home.

Severe Symptoms:

- Feeling agitated or disoriented.

- High temperature.

- Seizures.

- Ranting and violence.

- Hallucinations (visual) also known as delirium tremens.

There's no point in fudging this, it's going to be tough. A psychological issue comes in alongside these physical withdrawal symptoms. You may feel like there's no point in bothering, and have a little voice that tells you it's time to give up giving up. It's a very persuasive voice and many alcoholics who try to give up alone find they are not strong enough to resist it. It's easy to feel like withdrawal is far worse than drinking.

Above all, remember that it does get easier; the withdrawal symptoms are at their worst for a maximum of one week, often less, and after that things will start to get better. It's not just about giving up drinking, it's about rediscovering the world outside the bottle again, and this in itself can be hard. If it takes several goes to kick it, so what? Try not to let it get to you.

Don't give up. It's definitely better to quit than to keep drinking. Remember that you're trading this short period of misery for a longer, healthier life, so it's very much worth it.

Treating an Addiction

Very Severe Cases

Rehab will normally involve support groups, counselling or therapy (or both) and possibly medication. In the hospital or treatment centre you can expect to be kept in for some days. Only a very small number of people will require hospitalisation to deal with withdrawal symptoms for alcohol. You'll just need to buckle up for the ride, if you're part of that small minority, and trust the experts to take care of you.

You'll be in good hands and, as we've already discussed, it'll only last for a short while. If needed, medication like tranquilisers can be made available if you're hospitalised. You'll also be given fluids and electrolytes to replace lost minerals. The doctors will be monitoring things like your blood pressure, breathing and heart rate. The ongoing process of rehabilitation can be carried out at home, so you'll be released once the worst is over and you're physically stronger.

You'll be gaining an opportunity to learn to live your life to its fullest.

Those that go it alone are far more likely to fall off the wagon. Your chances of staying dry will be much higher the more support you're able to accept.

Those that go it alone are far more likely to fall off the wagon. Your chances of staying dry will be much higher the more support you're able to accept.

Quitting at Home

Alcohol affects natural sleeping patterns, and when you stop you will probably find you are very wakeful, being only able to sleep for a few hours at a time. Your doctor will be able to advise you on ways to avoid some of the physical effects such as shaking or restlessness and may prescribe beta blockers or sleeping tablets to help, but this will depend on each patient.

You might be anxious, irritable and restless, and you'll probably experience flu-like symptoms. The biggest danger for most recovering alcoholics is the psychological temptation to start drinking again, but most will be fine to stay at home while they quit drinking. Your resolve will be strengthened if you're able to get someone to keep an eye on you, and a good way to do this is to seek advice from your GP before giving up.

You're likely to find that the first three days will be the worst if you're giving up at home. You may have trouble getting to sleep. Eventually your natural rhythms will reassert themselves and you'll be able to get a good night's sleep. Just sleep when you're able to, and the rest of the time try to relax and watch TV or read a book.

Summing Up

- Giving up drinking will never be easy.

- Being prepared for withdrawal symptoms and challenges will make tackling this a little more doable.

- Whatever you do, try to stay positive.

- Try writing a list of all the reasons you want to stop drinking.

- The physical symptoms of withdrawal can be scary both for the person giving up and for the person looking after them. Try to be patient – it will get better.

- If you're in the supporting role whilst someone else is giving up, prepare yourself too.

- When you have dark days – and you will – remember the reasons for quitting.

- Cutting down before quitting can help; take time off work if you need it; make sure you have friends and family about and get some counselling or therapy.

- Even mild symptoms like cravings or anxiety are little fun, and the severe cases are going to be very uncomfortable.

10

The Recovery Options

Residential Treatments and Rehab

For those around a recovering alcoholic, knowing that the person is being taken care of in a residential treatment centre can give great peace of mind. Successful rehabilitation will depend largely on how much commitment and input the patient brings to it, although you can of course accept that this will go for the whole 'giving up' process; it's never going to be like falling off a log – there is hard work involved.

Well-worn or familiar drinking routines at home will remind you daily of the thing you're giving up, and rehab can give you time to break the habits and rediscover the old you, the sober you. Space and time to recover, with specialists on hand 24 hours a day can feel really safe, and be a positive way to address the issues. The rehab centres will offer structured support with counselling and therapy, not just dealing with breaking the addiction itself, but helping sufferers accept the change that life will undergo, and offering motivational support and ongoing treatment to help prevent relapsing.

In some cases, a big part of someone's success in giving up drinking can just come from having an opportunity to get away from it all. Private rehabilitation and residential treatment centres are pretty pricey, but well worth it if you can afford them. Rehabilitation centres can be a lifesaver, though they've become somewhat stigmatised by tabloid responses to troubled celebrities over the years.

Breaking the patterns of your everyday life can also make a massive difference. You'll be offered a specialised form of treatment if you attend a residential rehab unit. Fully-trained members of staff including therapists, security, counsellors and nurses will all be specialists in addiction management, so you'll be getting something a little more personal than general medical support.

Those normally tasked with looking after the person addicted to alcohol – the spouses, parents, children and partners – will be given an opportunity to let go of all the pain for a short while. As much as they love the person getting help, it can come as a welcome break.

Often a rehab centre will specialise in one or two particular types of addiction – alcohol is the most common and most centres will offer treatment for alcohol dependency cases.

Often a rehab centre will specialise in one or two particular types of addiction – alcohol is the most common and most centres will offer treatment for alcohol dependency cases. For the patient, rehab provides a chance to see how life is possible without their own particular band of poison, and an opportunity to face life without alcohol. They can also provide support in the challenge of relearning how to relate and talk to people again after a long period of drinking, as alcoholism can have a drastic effect on psychosocial skills.

For those with severe alcoholism and related conditions who can't afford to pay for private healthcare, there are options available through social services or the NHS. Many residential centres will have an option where you may be able to get some or all of the treatment funded by the state, but it will be means tested. In the case of alcohol-related crime, many criminal sentences will involve some kind of mandatory rehab term.

As a general rule, if you're able to afford treatment, you will be expected to pay for it.

How Rehab Works

All patients will need to be clean, sober and free from alcohol when they arrive at a rehabilitation centre. The centre will often try to involve the family of a recovering alcoholic, so that they understand the underlying principles of recovery and maintenance. First, however, the patient will have to get sober and go through the period of withdrawal and detoxification.

There is likely to be a search to make sure there are no hidden bottles, and the patient will have to sign a contract committing them to not drinking at all during their stay. If they roll up after "one last drink", they won't be accepted.

Staff at rehab centres are able to prescribe medication to assist with detoxing the system and managing any severe withdrawal symptoms. The cause of the dependency will need to be identified, so once these short-term prescriptions are dealt with the patient will be expected to start therapy and counselling to identify any underlying problems.

Can't Go for Residential Rehab?

All of the options – therapy, medication, etc – are available in the outside world too! Most people tackle alcoholism without residential rehab, and that's fine. It's a "luxury" not everyone can afford or access. At the end of the day, it doesn't matter where you are so long as you're committed and serious about getting sober.

Alcoholics Anonymous and the 12 Steps

While it's now widely used by groups like Narcotics Anonymous, a program for people addicted to drugs, and Al-Anon, a program for the friends and family of people with alcohol dependencies, the 12-Step method was originally made popular by AA (Alcoholics Anonymous). The programme has proved to be widely successful, with many of these groups basing themselves around the 12-Step method adapted to the support role, rather than being aimed at the sufferer.

Teens and older children with alcoholic parents can also access the steps through Alateen.

As set out by the AA, the 12 Steps are as follows:

1 We admitted we were powerless over alcohol - that our lives had become unmanageable.

2 Came to believe that a Power greater than ourselves could restore us to sanity.

3 Made a decision to turn our will and our lives over to the care of God as we understood Him.

4 Made a searching and fearless moral inventory of ourselves.

5 Admitted to God, to ourselves and to another human being the exact nature of our wrongs.

6 Were entirely ready to have God remove all these defects of character.

7 Humbly asked Him to remove our shortcomings.

8 Made a list of all persons we had harmed, and became willing to make amends to them all.

9 Made direct amends to such people wherever possible, except when to do so would injure them or others.

10 Continued to take personal inventory and when we were wrong promptly admitted it.

11 Sought through prayer and meditation to improve our conscious contact with God as we understood Him, praying only for knowledge of His will for us and the power to carry that out.

12 Having had a spiritual awakening as the result of these steps, we tried to carry this message to alcoholics and to practice these principles in all our affairs.

© **Copyright Alcoholics Anonymous. For more information on joining AA and the 12-Step method, visit www.alcoholics-anonymous.org.uk.**

Unfortunately, many people who are fully committed to giving up alcohol are put off the 12 Steps because of their overt religious overtones. It's clear that much of the programme is based very firmly in seeking spiritual guidance. It's very much about going on a journey of recovery and they do use words like 'fellowship' and 'reaching', which can be a bit uncomfortable for those who do not follow a similar belief system.

Alcoholics Anonymous have stated that they will still welcome anyone with open arms, even if they do not feel comfortable following the 12 Steps. Nobody will be forced to follow these guidelines.

Accepting these steps isn't a problem for some people. But for those who do have an issue with the way they're phrased, it can be helpful to think about the underlying meaning in each step. Removing the religious structure from most of the points is completely doable, and will allow you to tackle the programme without following beliefs you aren't comfortable with. For example, Step 1 is just about admitting that you have a problem, and Step 4 is about making an inventory of yourself. Steps 8-10 are about making amends. We can't deny AA's successful track record, though it's true that the 12 Steps aren't the right method for everyone.

All you can really do is aim to interpret the steps as best you can to suit your own beliefs, and try to keep an open mind.

AA point out that alcoholism is a disease with no cure, so they have a policy of total abstinence. There's no compromise. Giving up completely is the only way to control your addiction and stop it in its tracks.

You may well find a different group that suits you better – not all non-residential support has to be through the AA. Your doctor may be able to suggest some alternative groups in your area if you mention you aren't comfortable with the AA's system.

Help for Friends and Family

Remember that the alcoholic is going to need ongoing support too and you will need to be strong to cope. Living with an alcohol abuser can be very difficult and although you might be happy to see that person taking control and facing up to it, you will find all kinds of emotions welling up from years of unhappiness or strife in the home.

A big part of the alcoholic's rehabilitation will often be therapy. It could well be worth talking this over with your GP too, and asking for counselling or therapy on your own behalf. Those around the alcoholic will also be able to access support. There are support groups specifically for those around the alcoholic such as Al-Anon, or Alateen for younger members, which are both part of Alcoholics Anonymous.

Feelings of concern, resentment, devastation and anger are common in the family and friends of people with addictions. Nobody can expect you to let go of all negative emotions just because things are starting to get better. This is something you all have to go through together, and for that reason family therapy is highly recommended. It's also important that you're able to take up something that's just for you, to help you heal.

Look around and find out what support is available in your area, and you should find something that's right for you. Make sure you're looking after yourself, and don't underestimate just how much damage living with or around someone with an addiction can be. You need to nurture yourself and attend to your own needs. You're only human, after all.

Living with an alcohol abuser can be very difficult and although you might be happy to see that person taking control and facing up to it, you will find all kinds of emotions welling up from years of unhappiness or strife in the home.

Types of Therapy

You can access the recommended forms of therapy through Alcoholics Anonymous or your GP. This therapy will also be available to those who attend residential rehab centres.

Counselling (One on One)

Counselling differs from therapy in as much as it's more of a listening situation, with prompting, rather than deeper analysis or probing of the problem. This type of counselling gives you the opportunity to talk over problems to a sympathetic listener, one on one. Getting things off your chest is sometimes all you'll need.

Group Counselling

In this type of counselling, you'll get to share your experiences and emotions as part of a group. Knowing that there are others with similar problems can be a relief, and some people find this method very helpful. There are others who find the public aspect of this counselling challenging, though, and there's nothing wrong with that.

CBT (Cognitive Behavioural Therapy)

This therapy prods patients to remember, understand and resolve things, and to do it for themselves. Conscious intellectual activity is the focus here, as is indicated by the word "cognitive". It's a good way of getting to the root of the problem, though the process itself can be a bit of an emotional rollercoaster. You may be expected to discuss some painful memories or background.

Psychosocial Therapy

Psychosocial therapy will help a patient to redevelop those interpersonal skills needed to communicate with the outside world again. Many people find themselves unable to relate to people the way they used to when they become sober, as being drunk often means you're less accustomed to "normal" human interactions.

Marriage Counselling and Family Therapy

A huge role in recovery is often played by family and relationship counselling, as it goes without saying that the person dependant on alcohol is not the only person the addiction has damaged. Family members and close friends can experience some healing if they're helped to understand the condition better, and are given the opportunity to discuss fully the issues raised by the problem.

Summing Up

- Whether you can afford or qualify for residential care or not, the methods of rehabilitation you'll be using should be the same.

- The person with the addiction is not the only one who needs access to support and guidance.

- Anyone affected by this family illness is going to need a boost too, and rehab will apply to everybody involved, without exception.

- Detox, followed by counselling and therapy, will be the cornerstones for the recovery period, with ongoing counselling recommended to stay focused.

11

The Future

This Is It

I f you're reading this as an alcoholic, remember that once you've kicked the habit, then that's it – you need to accept that you cannot drink again.

It's much easier to start again than not, and resisting temptation is really hard. For each individual case, quitting drinking is going to raise different issues and unlock different experiences and emotions. Recovery tends to go a little more smoothly once the alcohol has passed the stage of cravings and withdrawal. And those around them will certainly find life is easier.

They're well on the way to rehabilitation at this stage, and should feel a lot better about themselves. Giving up alcohol is such a positive move, so the individual will have every right to feel really proud of themselves. This is a major achievement. Life as a sober person is always going to be better than life as a person addicted to alcohol, whatever level of behavioural issues and dependency there was before.

What we hope everyone will agree on at this point is that there's no going back. Whether the former drinker is feeling thankful and pleased to have sorted out their problem, proud to have conquered the beast or terrified of going back, they will hopefully acknowledge that life in recovery is better than life under the thumb of addiction.

There is no "odd drink" for someone with an addiction. Alcohol is something that needs to be taken seriously and, once you have recovered, avoided entirely. Taking even one drink is potentially disastrous, and would be such a waste after you've put so much work into getting sober.

Buddies

As a recovering addict moves through rehab, a buddy, or voluntary mentor, can be a great help. It's particularly good for those without close family to support them, as an addition to an already pressurised family unit, or perhaps for those who feel put off by groups. A buddy will be someone who has kicked the same habit and stuck to it, so they truly know the score.

Non-judgmental and a walking testimony to the fact that the habit can be licked, and stay licked, an addict in recovery can often really connect with a buddy, recognising that the buddy can completely understand what they're going through. If the recovering alcoholic falls off the wagon, they can call their buddy. A buddy is someone you can ring to talk about your experiences whenever you're struggling or feel tempted.

This type of support can be invaluable if you're getting help for an addiction. A buddy can make a real difference if you need to let off steam or are going through a rough period. They can often be much more helpful than family and friends, who will often have no real understanding of your ongoing battle and experiences, however sympathetic and well-meaning they may be.

It's not unusual to feel left out of the relationship that a recovering addict might have with their buddy if you're the spouse, or a close friend, of someone in recovery. It's easy to feel a little miffed when you realise you can't bond with the addict in the same way this relative stranger can. Just keep in mind how helpful this relationship can be, and try to focus on the outcome. It's important this relationship is allowed to develop if you want it to help with your loved one's addiction.

> Non-judgmental and a walking testimony to the fact that the habit can be licked, and stay licked, an addict in recovery can often really connect with a buddy, recognising that the buddy can completely understand what they're going through.

Replacing Alcohol

Take stock of where you are, and where you want to be. Removing the alcohol from your life is like opening the curtains and looking clearly at the room behind you, for the first time in a long time. The problems you had before you started drinking won't magically be solved when you stop drinking. Any emotional issues that you have that you previously dealt with by drinking will still be there, and may well be the root of your problem.

Marital and relationship issues will also be there if you haven't processed them properly. Deal with issues as you feel able, and don't overload yourself; what you're doing is tough and you should feel very proud of yourself for making the hardest decision in the first place – to give up. Gently dealing with these issues will be a big part of rehabilitation.

The idea is to help reduce your desire to drink in the future. Just try to take it one step at a time.

All of that said, sometimes one of the best parts of quitting is discovering that alcohol really was the root of all the other issues. Some people may have been living under the belief that they were inherently unemployable, insane, stupid or violent, and that there was just something really wrong with them. It can be a real relief to find out that without alcohol, you're a perfectly healthy, functional human being.

It's a definite factor that the time normally spent drinking is now going to be empty. There will have been a whole lot of each day taken up with the pastime of drinking, and finding something else to fill that time is important. Get busy! Apart from removing temptation, it works on many other levels. Very common is for recovered alcoholics to go into support care themselves and become counsellors or buddies – but this could be way down the line when the habit is well under control.

Reevaluating your life is a good thing to do right now. You have choices now that were never available to you when you were drinking.

Exposing yourself to places and people who you previously associated solely with alcohol, or having no plans for what to do at the times of the day when you used to drink, can be dangerous. If someone offers you a drink, know in advance what you're going to say. Many people recovering from alcohol dependency relapse as a result of these unprotected weak spots. Being prepared is so, so important.

Get rid of all the alcohol in your house if you're trying to support someone's recovery. You don't need it either – tip the stuff down the sink! It's a great way to show respect and solidarity.

Re-training and looking into new careers can also be a good idea if you're recovering from alcoholism. Habits are hard to break, and you may have lived your life immersed in alcohol for a long time. Rome wasn't built in a day, and if you've had a long term or obsessive relationship with alcohol, giving up isn't going to be like clicking your fingers. Your previous addiction is just looking for an opportunity to knock on the door again, so it's important that you try and find something to do as soon as you're strong enough.

Find something that will keep you away from the pub.

One Day at a Time

If you wake up feeling positive, and go to bed each day without falling by the wayside, you can give yourself a massive pat on the back, because only you will appreciate how hard just doing that is some days.

If you wake up feeling positive, and go to bed each day without falling by the wayside, you can give yourself a massive pat on the back, because only you will appreciate how hard just doing that is some days. Each day will make you stronger, and there will come a time when you don't have slip ups and you are strong. But if you make mistakes and have slip ups, don't lose heart.

Being realistic is the most important thing you can do right now. It takes time to recover fully from something like alcoholism and while making the decision to quit is the biggest part, the long-term work is equally vital. Keep in mind that this is something you need to take on one day at a time, and face each challenge as it comes.

A certain gene is used to break down alcohol in the liver, and there are drugs available that replicate that process. The gene causes nausea, palpitations and flushing, and occurs naturally in some people. Alcohol toleration in these people is much lower than in those who don't have the gene. If you're seriously worried about being able to say no to alcohol, you can take a drug to create this reaction pharmaceutically, which can be helpful for some people.

It's fine to struggle. Everyone makes mistakes once in a while, so if you slip just haul yourself back up and try again. So long as you don't let drinking become the default again, you still have a shot at recovery. Just take things one day at a time for now.

Summing Up

- Look ahead to a future without alcohol, and try to remain optimistic.

- You'll feel tempted some days. This is unavoidable. Some days, you might even give into temptation. But things will get better if you just keep at it.

- Be forgiving of yourself, and try not to get upset when things go wrong. Take it slowly, and accept the support of others. This will be a massive challenge, and you should be really proud of yourself for making it this far. When the drinking is behind you, things will be so much better.

- If you're not the alcoholic, but the carer or supporting family, remember this: it's a huge and frightening step and mistakes will happen.

- Your whole life stretches before you, and taking this step towards a brighter, sober existence can only be a good thing.

Help List

General Information

Alcoholics Anonymous
www.alcoholics-anonymous.org.uk
Address: PO Box 1, 10 Toft Green, York, YO1 7ND
Tel.: 0800 9177 650
Alcoholics Anonymous are a worldwide organisation who aim to help people give up drinking through regular meetings and support groups. Find groups in your area and information on how they work on their website.

Alcohol Change
alcoholchange.org.uk
Address: Alcohol Change UK, 27 Swinton Street, London WC1X 9NW
Tel.: 020 3907 8480
Email: contact@alcoholchange.org.uk
Alcohol Change UK is a new charity formed by the merger of Alcohol Concern and Alcohol Research UK. Their new website combines the content from these two charities along with their former Welsh site, Drink Wise Wales.

Alcohol Focus Scotland
www.alcohol-focus-scotland.org.uk
Address: 2nd Floor, 166 Buchanan Street, Glasgow, G1 2LW
Tel.: 0141 572 6700
Email: enquiries@alcohol-focus-scotland.org.uk
Scotland's national voluntary organisation offering information and advice about responsible drinking. The website contains a range of downloadable leaflets and provides information and training on alcohol related issues.

British Liver Trust

www.britishlivertrust.org.uk

Address: 6 Dean Park Crescent, Bournemouth BH1 1HL

Tel.: 01425 481320   Helpline: 0800 652 7330

Email: info@britishlivertrust.org.uk

The British Liver Trust support patients and families so nobody has to face liver disease alone. They're campaigning to improve awareness so more people are aware of the risks to the liver, and are lobbying for improved services for patients.

Department of Health and Social Care

https://www.gov.uk/government/organisations/department-of-health-and-social-care

Address: Ministerial Correspondence and Public Enquiries Unit, Department of Health and Social Care, 39 Victoria Street, London SW1H 0EU, United Kingdom

Tel: 0207 210 4850

Supports ministers in leading the nation's health and social care to help people live more independent, healthier lives for longer.

Down Your Drink

www.downyourdrink.org.uk

Originally run by Alcohol Concern, the Down Your Drink program is for people who are worried about their drinking. It allows you to find out if you're drinking too much and access online support if necessary.

Drinkaware

www.drinkaware.co.uk

Address: Finsbury Circus (Salisbury House), 3rd Floor (Room 519), London EC2M 5QQ

Tel.: 020 7766 9900

Email: contact@drinkaware.co.uk

This was set up in 2006 by the Portman Group to improve public awareness and understanding of responsible drinking. On the website you'll find useful information about alcohol and drinking, and practical tips and facts to help you become more drink aware. A drink diary is included.

Drinkline

Tel.: 0300 123 1110

Drinkline is the national alcohol helpline. You can call their free confidential helpline if you're worried about your drinking or someone else's. It's open on weekdays from 9AM to 8PM, and weekends from 11AM to 4PM.

Drinksafely

www.drinksafely.soton.ac.uk

Email: nick.sheron@soton.ac.uk

The liver team at Southampton University Hospitals Trust (SUHT) have created this informational website to inform drinkers of the risks surrounding alcohol. They have a great "Drinkulator" calculator, which can show you if the amount you drink is dangerous to your health.

Food and Drink Federation (FDF)

www.fdf.org.uk

T. 020 7836 2460

F. 020 7836 0580

Post: 6th Floor, 10 Bloomsbury Way, London WC1A 2SL

The Food and Drink Federation (FDF) is the voice of the UK food and drink industry, the largest manufacturing sector in the country.

FRANK

www.talktofrank.com

Tel.: 0800 77 66 00

Email: frank@talktofrank.com

Also known as The National Drugs Helpline, FRANK has a freephone helpline and a website that offers "honest information about drugs."

GOV.UK

www.gov.uk

This is the best place to find information about government services in your area.

Lancet

www.thelancet.com

Address: 125 London Wall, London EC2Y 5AS

Tel: +44 (0) 207 424 4950 (Lancet Journal Office)

Email: editorial@lancet.com (general editorial enquiries)

The UK's leading medical journal, which has loads of articles you'll find interesting and helpful.

National Organisation for Foetal Alcohol Syndrome-UK (NOFAS UK)

www.nofas-uk.org

Address: 022 China Works, 100 Black Prince Road, Lambeth, London SE1 7SJ

Tel.: 0208 458 5951   Urgent calls: 07920 747 560

Email: help@nofas-uk.org

NOFAS UK are a charity dedicated to providing information and guidance to families and children affected by Foetal Alcohol Syndrome.

NHS Health Scotland
www.healthscotland.scot
Address: Gyle Square, 1 South Gyle Crescent, Edinburgh EH12 9EB
Tel.: 0141 414 2888
Email: publications@health.scot.nhs.uk
Health Scotland publishes information leaflets and leads education campaigns on health issues aimed at the Scottish public. Their publications section contains factsheets, leaflets and booklets on a wide range of health issues, including those around alcohol.

Patient
patient.info
Patient are working to empower everyone to take control of their own health. They aim to help people feel better and live longer by providing reliable clinical information written and reviewed by a broad network of doctors and healthcare professionals.

Work & Employment

ACAS
www.acas.org.uk
"ACAS (Advisory, Conciliation and Arbitration Service) provides free and impartial information and advice to employers and employees on all aspects of workplace relations and employment law. We support good relationships between employers and employees which underpin business success. But when things go wrong we help by providing conciliation to resolve workplace problems."

NHS Sites for Different Areas of the UK

These are useful gateway sites to access in depth information and support relevant to the area where you live. Scotland, Northern Ireland, England and Wales all have different NHS sites, which you can find below. Through these you will be able to find information about what's going on in your local area. Available treatments as well as information on healthy living and medical facts about the causes and effects of alcoholism can be found on each website.
England: www.nhs.uk
Northern Ireland: http://online.hscni.net/
Scotland: www.show.scot.nhs.uk
Wales: www.wales.nhs.uk
Healthcare Improvement Scotland (NHS QIS)

www.nhshealthquality.org
General queries and feedback: comments.his@nhs.net
Tel: 0131 623 4300
Edinburgh office: Gyle Square, 1 South Gyle Crescent, Edinburgh EH12 9EB
Glasgow office: Delta House, 50 West Nile Street, Glasgow G1 2NP
Set up to improve quality of care and treatment delivered by NHS Scotland.

Support for Families and Professionals

Al-Anon UK
www.al-anonuk.org.uk
Head Office
Address: Al-Anon Family Groups UK & Eire, 57B Great Suffolk Street, London SE1 0BB
Tel.: 020 7593 2070
Email: Contact form on website.
Republic of Ireland
Address: Al-Anon Information Centre, Room 5, 5 Capel Street, Dublin 1, EIRE
Tel.: 00353 01 873 2699 (Helpline 10.30am – 2.30pm, Mon – Fri)
Email: info@alanon.ie
Northern Ireland
Address: Peace House, 224 Lisburn Road, Belfast, BT9 6GE
Tel.: 028 9068 2368 (Helpline 10am – 1pm, Mon – Fri/ 6pm – 11pm, 7 days a week)
Al-Anon aim to support the family and friends of those who are giving up drinking by providing meetings and support group. They believe that recovery can be made easier if we change our attitudes to this family illness.

Alateen
www.al-anonuk.org.uk/alateen
Tel.: 020 7593 2070
Part of Al-Anon, this organisation offers support to younger family members (aged 12 to 17) affected by a problem drinker.

Carers Trust

www.carers.org

Address: 32-36 Loman Street, London SE1 0EH

Tel: 0300 772 9600

Email: info@carers.org

"Carers Trust is a major charity for, with and about carers."

They're working to improve the services, information and support available to those who provide unpaid care to friends and family members who are unable to care for themselves.

Families Anonymous

www.famanon.org.uk

Address: Families Anonymous, Doddington & Rollo Community Association, Charlotte Despard Avenue, Battersea, London SW11 5HD

Tel.: 0207 4984 680

Email: office@famanon.org.uk

Families Anonymous (Famanon) is a self-help organisation for the families of people who abuse drugs. There may well be a FA support group running in your area.

Family Lives (Parentline Plus)

www.familylives.org.uk

Address: 15-17 The Broadway, Hatfield, Hertfordshire AL9 5HZ

Tel.: 020 7553 3080

Family Lives works to build a stronger society by transforming the lives of families, strengthening relationships and supporting parents. They have trained family support workers (paid and voluntary) who can offer any family immediate and ongoing help online, in person or on the phone.

Includem

www.includem.org

Address: Includem, Head Office, Unit 6000, Academy Office Park, Gower Street, Glasgow, G51 1PR

Tel.: 0141 427 0523

Email: enquiries@includem.co.uk

Includem works with socially excluded young people, care leavers and young offenders in many areas of Scotland. It covers a wide range of issues, including misuse of alcohol.

Institute of Alcohol Studies

www.ias.org.uk

Address: Alliance House, 12 Caxton Street, London SW1h 0QS

Tel.: 020 7222 4001

Email: info@ias.org.uk

The Institute of Alcohol Studies is an independent organisation working to improve society's awareness and understanding of alcohol-related issues. You can find lots of helpful factsheets on their website.

Kids Health

www.kidshealth.org

This US online magazine has some useful advice for teenagers. There are articles on how to cope with an alcoholic parent and what to do if you've got an alcohol problem yourself.

The Medical Council on Alcohol (MCA)

www.m-c-a.org.uk/Home/home

Address: 5 St Andrews Place, London NW1 4LB

Tel.: 020 7487 4445

Email: aline.oshima@m-c-a.org.uk

The Medical Council on Alcohol (MCA) is a charity which focuses on the education of medical and allied professionals on the effects of alcohol on our health. Their website is a great resource for professionals, with links to journals and publications and contact details for regional advisors.

Mentor UK

mentoruk.org.uk

Address: 60 St Martin's Lane, London WC2N 4JS

Tel.: 0203 963 2715

Email: admin@mentoruk.org

Mentor UK works to prevent drug-related harm in children and young people. It supports those working with young people to find the best ways to implement effective drug prevention initiatives.

The National Association for Children of Alcoholics (NACOA)

www.nacoa.org.uk

Address: PO Box 64, Fishponds, Bristol, BS16 2UH

Tel.: 0800 358 3456

Email: helpline@nacoa.org.uk

The National Association for Children of Alcoholics works with the children (both young and grown up) of alcoholics, providing them with advice and help. Those concerned about children's welfare can also find useful information here.

Portman Group

www.portmangroup.org.uk

Address: 4th Floor, 20 Conduit Street, London W1S 2XW

Tel.: 020 7290 1460

Email: info@portmangroup.org.uk

Established in 1989, The Portman Group is supported by the UK's leading drink producers to help promote sensible drinking. Their role is to encourage and challenge the industry to promote its products responsibly.

Priory

www.priorygroup.com

Address: Priory Group Head Office, Floor 5, Hammersmith Road, London W14 8UD

Tel.: 0207 605 0910

Email: info@priorygroup.com

Priory is a leading independent provider of information, behavioural care and health services, working with alcohol-related issues among other fields. They aim to help people achieve their maximum potential by taking control of their lives.

Release

www.release.org.uk

Address: 61 Mansell Street, London E1 8AN

Tel.: 020 7324 2989

Email: ask@release.org.uk

Release offers a range of specialist services to professionals and the public concerning drugs, including information on alcohol. They give advice to drug users, their families, friends and statutory and voluntary agencies.

Drug Information

Action on Addiction

www.actiononaddiction.org.uk

Address: East Knoyle, Wiltshire, SP3 6BE

Tel.: 0300 330 0659

Email: enquiries@actiononaddiction.org.uk

Action on Addiction provides training, research, family support, information and treatment with the goal of disarming and beating addiction. Their website has some great resources and links for recovery and treatment options.

Addaction

www.addaction.org.uk
Address: Part Lower Ground Floor, Gate House, 1-3 St. John's Square, London EC1M 4DH
Tel.: 0207 251 5860
Email: info@addaction.org.uk
UK treatment agency offering support to recovering addicts plus families and communities to cope with the effects of drug and alcohol misuse.

Adfam

www.adfam.org.uk
Address: Adfam, 2nd Floor, 120 Cromer Street, London WC1H 8BS
Tel.: 020 3817 9410
Email: admin@adfam.org.uk
Adfam's website provides advice and information, including a list of local family support services, for the families of drug and alcohol users. They can signpost you to local support services. Adfam also provide training, outreach work and publications.

DrugScope

www.drugscope.org.uk
Address: DrugScope, 4th Floor, Asra House, 1 Long Lane, London SE1 4PG
Tel.: 020 7234 9730
Email: info@drugscope.org.uk
DrugScope provides information and resources for professionals and the public on drug-related issues. It provides an online encyclopaedia of drugs and a directory of help sources.

Scottish Drugs Forum (SDF)

www.sdf.org.uk
Address: 91 Mitchell Street, Glasgow, G1 3LN
Tel.: Tel: 0141 221 1175
Email: enquiries@sdf.org.uk
This is a drugs policy and information agency co-ordinating effective response to drug use in Scotland. SDF aims to support and represent, at both local and national levels, a wide range of interests, promoting collaborative, evidence-based responses to drug use.

UKNA (Narcotics Anonymous in the UK)

www.ukna.org

Tel.: 0300 999 1212

Email: ukpi@ukna.org

UKNA provide information for professionals working with addicts seeking recovery, for people who feel they may have a drug problem, and for recovering addicts. Contact numbers and email addresses for NA regional offices in the UK and the rest of the world can be found on the website.

Sexual Health

NHS – Good Sex Tips

www.nhs.uk/live-well/sexual-health/good-sex-tips/

A page on the NHS website about having a good sex life in a safe, healthy way.

Rape Crisis England & Wales

www.rapecrisis.org.uk

Address: Suite E4, Josephs Well, Hanover Walk, Leeds, LS3 1AB

Email: rcewinfo@rapecrisis.org.uk

This website provides information for victims of sexual violence, their friends and families. Use the map provided to find details of local rape crisis groups. A comprehensive list of contacts and links is provided.

Sources

Alcohol-specific deaths in the UK - Office for National Statistics
**https://www.ons.gov.uk/peoplepopulationandcommunity/healthandsocialcare/
causesofdeath/bulletins/alcoholrelateddeathsintheunitedkingdom/registeredin2017**
Alcohol and drugs misuse | Department of Health
https://www.health-ni.gov.uk/articles/alcohol-and-drugs-misuse
Alcohol statistics | Alcohol Change UK
https://alcoholchange.org.uk/alcohol-facts/fact-sheets/alcohol-statistics
Binge-drinker children pour into hospitals | Society | The Guardian
https://www.theguardian.com/society/2003/aug/24/drugsandalcohol.medicineandhealth
New alcohol guidelines: How much is 14 units? | The Independent
**https://www.independent.co.uk/life-style/health-and-families/health-news/new-alcohol-
guidelines-how-many-drinks-is-14-units-a6802091.html**
Roxxoff fights back
https://www.morningadvertiser.co.uk/Article/2003/08/28/Roxxoff-fights-back
Smoking, Drinking and Drug Use Among Young People in England - 2016 - NHS Digital –
**https://digital.nhs.uk/data-and-information/publications/statistical/smoking-drinking-and-
drug-use-among-young-people-in-england/2016**
Teenage drinking | Drinkaware
https://www.drinkaware.co.uk/advice/underage-drinking/teenage-drinking
The quiet death of the alcopop - BBC News
https://www.bbc.co.uk/news/magazine-23502892
UK Underage Consumption | Drinkaware
https://www.drinkaware.co.uk/research/data/uk-underage-consumption